Mastering Algorithms: From Theory to Practice

A Complete Guide to Problem Solving, Design Patterns, and Computational Thinking

By

George Keil

First Edition
2026

Preface

Algorithms are the invisible engines of the modern world. They determine how information flows, how decisions are made, how resources are allocated, and how problems are solved at scales far beyond human capability. From the moment we unlock a smartphone to the systems that manage transportation, finance, healthcare, and communication, algorithms are constantly at work, shaping our experiences in ways that are often unnoticed yet profoundly influential.

This book was written to make algorithms visible, understandable, and meaningful. Rather than treating algorithms as isolated mathematical objects or language-specific code fragments, this book presents them as *ideas* structured ways of thinking about problems. It emphasizes why algorithms exist, how they are designed, what tradeoffs they involve, and how they behave in real systems.

The material progresses from foundational concepts to advanced and emerging topics, reflecting how algorithmic thinking itself develops. Early chapters focus on intuition, problem-solving strategies, and efficiency analysis. Later chapters explore algorithms that operate under uncertainty, scale across distributed systems, learn from data, and influence society at large. Throughout, the goal is not memorization, but understanding.

This book is intended for students, educators, and practitioners who want a coherent and modern view of algorithms. It assumes curiosity rather than prior mastery. Mathematical ideas are introduced carefully and always connected to practical relevance. Visual reasoning, real-world case studies, and reflective questions are used to reinforce learning and encourage deeper engagement.

Algorithms are not static truths. They evolve with hardware, data, and societal needs. By the end of this book, the reader should not only understand existing algorithms, but also feel equipped to evaluate new ones, question their impact, and design solutions responsibly. That is the deeper purpose of algorithmic literacy, and it is the guiding spirit of this work.

Acknowledgement

No book is written in isolation, and this one is no exception. Its ideas are shaped by centuries of mathematical thought, decades of computer science research, and the collective efforts of educators, engineers, and researchers who continue to refine how algorithms are understood and applied.

I would like to acknowledge the pioneers of algorithmic thinking whose work laid the foundations for this field. Their insights transformed abstract reasoning into systematic computation and made it possible to formalize problem solving in ways that continue to influence modern technology.

I am grateful to teachers and mentors, both formal and informal, whose explanations, examples, and insistence on clarity helped shape the perspective reflected in this book. Their emphasis on understanding over rote learning remains an enduring influence.

I also acknowledge the global open-source and academic communities whose shared knowledge, tools, and discussions make learning algorithms a collaborative endeavor rather than a solitary pursuit. Many of the ideas presented here have been refined through collective exploration rather than individual discovery.

Finally, this book is written with the learner in mind. Every reader who struggles with a concept, asks a deeper question, or seeks to apply algorithms thoughtfully is part of the reason this work exists. If this book helps even a small number of readers see algorithms more clearly and use them more responsibly, then it has fulfilled its purpose.

Introduction

Algorithms are systematic procedures for solving problems. At their simplest, they resemble everyday activities: following a recipe, assembling furniture, or finding the fastest route to a destination. At their most sophisticated, they coordinate millions of machines, analyze vast streams of data, and assist in decisions that affect entire societies. Despite this range, all algorithms share a common goal: transforming input into output through a finite, well-defined sequence of steps.

Computer science is often described as the study of algorithms, but this description is incomplete without context. Algorithms are not just about correctness. They are about efficiency, scalability, reliability, and impact. An algorithm that works for ten inputs may fail for a million. An algorithm that is fast may be unfair. An algorithm that is accurate may be opaque. Understanding algorithms therefore requires more than knowing *how* they work. It requires understanding *when* they work, *why* they work, and *what consequences they produce*.

This book introduces algorithms as tools for reasoning about complexity and structure. It begins with the development of algorithmic thinking, showing how problems can be decomposed, abstracted, and systematically solved. It then explores core algorithmic strategies such as divide and conquer, greedy methods, dynamic programming, and backtracking. These strategies form a mental toolkit that reappears across domains.

As the book progresses, the scope expands. Algorithms are examined in contexts where data is uncertain, incomplete, or continuously streaming. They are studied in environments where computation must be distributed, decisions must be made in real time, or exact solutions are impractical. The later chapters confront the ethical and societal dimensions of algorithmic systems, recognizing that technical decisions increasingly carry moral weight.

This is not a book about any single programming language, nor is it a catalog of code snippets. Code is used where necessary, but the emphasis remains on ideas that transcend syntax. The intent is to build transferable understanding rather than narrow technical proficiency.

Algorithms are among humanity's most powerful intellectual creations. They allow us to extend reasoning beyond individual limits and to operate at scales that would otherwise be impossible. Learning algorithms, therefore, is not only a technical exercise. It is an invitation to think more clearly, design more responsibly, and engage more thoughtfully with the systems that shape the modern world.

1. The Algorithmic Mindset

Imagine you are cooking your favorite meal for the first time. You open a recipe and begin to follow it step by step. First, you gather the ingredients. Then you preheat the oven, chop the vegetables, season the dish, and cook it for a precise amount of time. If you skip a step, do things out of order, or guess randomly, the result is unpredictable. But when you follow the steps carefully, the dish turns out just as expected.

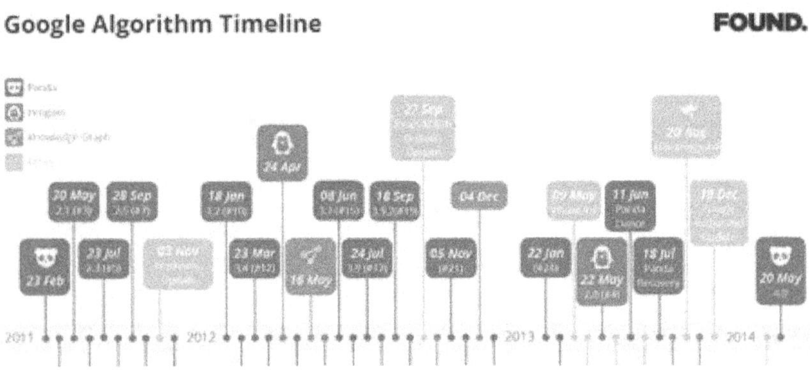

Without realizing it, you are executing an algorithm.

Algorithms are not mysterious lines of code hidden inside computers. They are structured ways of thinking, planning, and solving problems. Every time you follow driving directions, assemble furniture, or search for a contact on your phone, you are relying on algorithms some written down, some memorized, some performed instinctively.

This book begins with a simple but powerful idea: algorithms are everywhere, and learning how they work changes how you understand both computers and the world around you.

From Everyday Life to Computational Thinking

Consider navigating to a new place in an unfamiliar city. You might open a GPS app, type in your destination, and follow the directions it provides. The app evaluates multiple routes, considers traffic conditions, estimates travel time, and selects the best path. All of this happens in seconds, but underneath that simplicity lies a carefully designed algorithm deciding what "best" means.

Even without technology, you solve similar problems daily. When you look for a book on a shelf, you might scan left to right. When the shelf is alphabetized, you naturally jump closer to where the author's name should be. When it is not, you check one book at a time. Each approach is a different algorithm, with different efficiency.

This way of breaking down tasks into clear, repeatable steps is called algorithmic thinking. It means defining a problem precisely, identifying the inputs you have, the output you want, and the process that reliably transforms one into the other.

Before computers ever existed, humans were already thinking this way.

A Brief History of Algorithms

More than two thousand years ago, the Greek mathematician Euclid described a step-by-step method for finding the greatest common divisor of two numbers. Today, this method is still taught as the Euclidean Algorithm and remains one of the oldest known algorithms still in use.

Centuries later, in the 9th century, a Persian scholar named Al-Khwarizmi wrote influential texts describing systematic methods for solving mathematical problems. His name gave rise to the word algorithm itself, a linguistic reminder that structured problem-solving long predates modern machines.

What changed with computers was not the invention of algorithms, but their scale and speed. Machines can execute millions or billions of steps in the time it takes a human to blink. This makes the quality of an algorithm how efficient, accurate, and scalable it is critically important.

Today, algorithms power search engines, recommendation systems, financial markets, medical diagnostics, and navigation tools. They quietly shape what information we see, which routes we travel, and how decisions are made at global scale.

What Makes an Algorithm "Good"?

Not all algorithms are created equal. Two algorithms can solve the same problem and still differ dramatically in usefulness.

A good algorithm is correct, meaning it produces the right output for all valid inputs. It is also clear, so that others can understand and implement it. Beyond correctness, efficiency becomes essential. An algorithm that works well for ten items but fails for a million is often impractical in the real world.

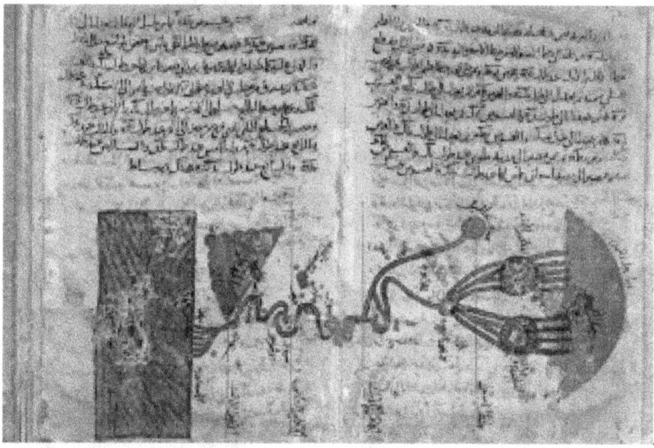

A good algorithm is also finite, meaning it eventually stops, and general, meaning it solves not just one instance of a problem but an entire class of similar problems. Perhaps most importantly, a good algorithm reflects thoughtful design: it anticipates edge cases, handles unexpected inputs gracefully, and balances simplicity with performance.

As this book progresses, you will learn how computer scientists analyze algorithms not just by whether they work, but by how well they scale as problems grow larger.

Think About It

At the grocery store, how do you decide which checkout line to join? Do you choose the shortest line, the fastest cashier, or the line with the fewest items? You are applying an informal algorithm. Ask yourself what assumptions you are making, and when those assumptions might fail.

A Case Study: How Search Engines Find Information

When you type a question into a search engine, the result feels almost magical. In less than a second, millions of web pages are evaluated and ranked. But no magic is involved only algorithms.

Behind the scenes, search engines rely on complex systems that crawl the web, index content, and evaluate relevance. They use algorithms to match your query to documents, estimate usefulness, and rank results. Factors such as keyword relevance, page structure, freshness, and authority all play a role.

Early search engines relied heavily on simple keyword matching. Modern systems go much further, incorporating language understanding, user intent, and context. Even so, the core challenge remains the same: given an enormous collection of data, how do you find the most relevant information quickly?

This is one of the central problems of computer science, and it illustrates why algorithmic thinking matters. A poorly designed search algorithm would be slow, inaccurate, or easily manipulated. A well-designed one transforms overwhelming amounts of data into usable knowledge.

Throughout this book, search engines will reappear as a recurring example, showing how foundational ideas searching, sorting, optimization, and graph traversal combine to solve real-world problems at scale.

Quick Exercise

Write down the steps you follow when searching for a lost item at home. Do you start in the last place you remember seeing it? Do you check the most likely locations first? Try rewriting your process as a numbered set of instructions. You have just designed an algorithm.

Looking Ahead

This chapter introduced algorithms not as abstract formulas, but as a way of thinking that connects daily life to computation. In the chapters that follow, you will learn how to express algorithms precisely, analyze their efficiency, and design increasingly powerful solutions to complex problems.

The journey begins not with code, but with mindset and once you start thinking algorithmically, you may never look at ordinary problems the same way again.

2. Computational Problem Solving

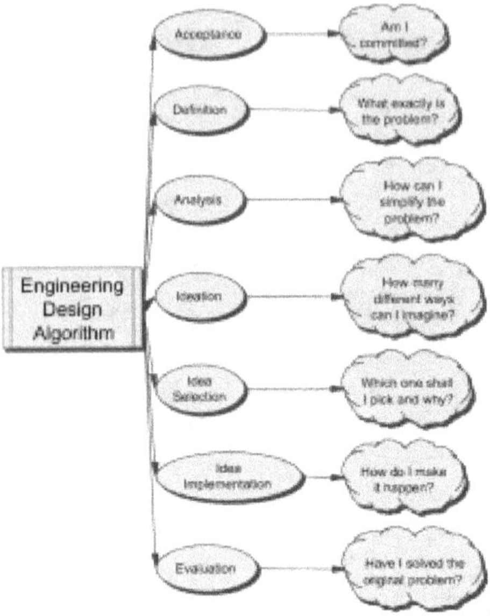

Learning algorithms is not primarily about memorizing techniques or writing code quickly. It is about learning how to **think clearly in the presence of complexity**. Many beginners struggle not because the problems are impossible, but because the problems feel overwhelming when viewed all at once. Computational problem solving provides a structured way to move from confusion to clarity, step by step, with confidence.

In this chapter, you will learn a repeatable framework that professionals use to approach complex problems. The framework consists of four stages: decomposition, pattern recognition, abstraction, and algorithm design. These stages are not rigid rules but guiding principles that help transform vague problems into precise solutions. To make these ideas concrete, we will return repeatedly to a single running example: planning a road trip. Along the way, we will examine common beginner mistakes with empathy and explore how real-world systems such as GPS navigation apply these same principles at scale.

Why Structure Matters in Problem Solving

When people first encounter computational problems, they often try to jump directly to a solution. This usually leads to frustration, because the mind attempts to hold too many details at once. Computers succeed at problem solving not because they are intelligent in a human sense, but because they follow carefully structured instructions without distraction or ambiguity.

Structured problem solving allows humans to work in a similar way. By breaking a problem into smaller pieces, recognizing similarities with known problems, ignoring irrelevant details, and then designing a clear procedure, even very complex challenges become manageable. This process does not remove creativity; instead, it gives creativity a stable foundation.

Professional software engineers, data scientists, and system designers use this structured approach constantly, whether they are building navigation systems, scheduling airline flights, or optimizing search engines. The difference between beginners and experts is not talent, but practice with this way of thinking.

The Four-Step Framework

Computational problem solving can be understood as a cycle rather than a straight line. You may move back and forth between steps as your understanding improves, but the overall flow remains consistent.

The first step is **decomposition**, where you break a large problem into smaller, more manageable subproblems. The second step is **pattern recognition**, where you identify similarities between this problem and problems you have seen before. The third step is **abstraction**, where you focus on what truly matters and temporarily ignore unnecessary details. The final step is **algorithm design**, where you create a clear, step-by-step solution.

To see how these steps work together, we will apply them to a familiar situation before moving to more technical examples.

Running Example: Planning a Road Trip

Imagine you are planning a road trip from your home to a city several hundred kilometers away. At first glance, the problem feels large and vague. You need to decide when to leave, which route to take, where to stop, how much fuel you will need, and how long the trip will take. Trying to solve everything at once quickly becomes overwhelming.

Decomposition

The first step is to break the problem into parts. You might separate it into route planning, time estimation, fuel management, and rest stops. Each of these subproblems can then be considered independently, making the overall task feel far less intimidating.

Pattern Recognition

Next, you recognize that you have planned trips before. You know that highways are usually faster than city roads, that traffic is heavier during certain hours, and that rest stops tend to appear at regular intervals. These patterns help you avoid starting from zero and allow you to reuse prior knowledge.

Abstraction

At this stage, you ignore details that do not matter yet. The color of your car or the music you will play does not affect route optimization, so those details can be set aside. You focus instead on distances, speeds, and road types, which are the variables that influence travel time.

Algorithm Design

Finally, you create a step-by-step plan. You might decide to select the fastest route, estimate travel time based on average speed, schedule stops every two hours, and adjust the plan if traffic conditions change. This plan is an algorithm, even though you may never write it down formally.

How GPS Systems Apply the Same Principles

Modern GPS systems, such as those used by **Google Maps**, apply the same framework on a massive scale. The system decomposes the problem into mapping the road network, estimating travel times, and responding to real-time traffic data. It recognizes patterns from historical traffic behavior, abstracts away irrelevant information such as road color or signage design, and then applies sophisticated algorithms to compute optimal routes.

What feels like a simple suggestion on your phone is the result of decades of refinement in computational problem solving. Understanding this process helps demystify technology and shows that professional solutions are built from the same logical steps you are learning now.

Common Pitfall: Trying to Solve Everything at Once

One of the most common beginner mistakes is attempting to design a complete solution immediately. This often leads to confusion and self-doubt. When you feel stuck, it is usually a sign that decomposition has not gone far enough. Taking time to break the problem into smaller pieces is not a weakness; it is a professional habit.

Practice Problem 1: Organizing a Study Schedule

Consider the task of creating a weekly study schedule. Begin by decomposing the problem into subjects, available time slots, and priorities. Look for patterns in your energy levels during the day. Abstract away distractions such as exact locations and focus on time blocks. Then design a simple algorithm that assigns subjects to time slots based on priority and availability.

Reflect on how much easier the task feels once it is structured.

Practice Problem 2: Finding a Book in a Library

Imagine searching for a specific book in a large library. Decompose the task into identifying the section, locating the shelf, and scanning the books. Recognize patterns such as alphabetical ordering. Abstract away book cover designs and focus on titles or call numbers. Design a step-by-step search strategy and compare it to how a librarian might approach the same problem.

Common Pitfall: Confusing Details with Importance

Beginners often fixate on details that do not affect the solution. This can slow progress and increase frustration. Abstraction is a skill that improves with practice, and it involves making conscious decisions about what to ignore, not guessing.

Practice Problem 3: Planning a Budget

For a monthly budget, decompose expenses into fixed and variable categories. Recognize patterns in recurring payments. Abstract away individual purchase brands and focus on total amounts. Design an algorithm that allocates income to expenses and savings in a consistent way.

Practice Problem 4: Sorting Photos on a Phone

Imagine organizing thousands of photos. Decompose the task into grouping by date, location, or event. Recognize patterns such as repeated locations or faces. Abstract away file sizes and focus on metadata. Design a step-by-step process for sorting that could be automated.

Practice Problem 5: Estimating Delivery Time

Suppose you are estimating delivery time for an online order. Decompose the process into processing, shipping, and local delivery. Recognize patterns from previous orders. Abstract away packaging details and focus on distance and speed. Design an algorithm that produces a reasonable estimate under uncertainty.

Common Pitfall: Expecting Perfect Solutions

Another beginner mistake is believing that algorithms must always produce perfect answers. In reality, many real-world algorithms aim for solutions that are good enough and improve over time. GPS routes, for example, are constantly adjusted as new information becomes available.

Reflection: Thinking Like a Problem Solver

At its core, computational problem solving is about developing patience and clarity. By slowing down, structuring your thinking, and embracing iteration, you train yourself to approach problems systematically rather than emotionally. This mindset applies far beyond computer science, influencing how you plan projects, make decisions, and adapt to uncertainty.

As you move forward in this book, these four steps will appear again and again, sometimes explicitly and sometimes in the background. With practice, they will become second nature, and complex problems will begin to feel not intimidating, but inviting.

3. Expressing Algorithms

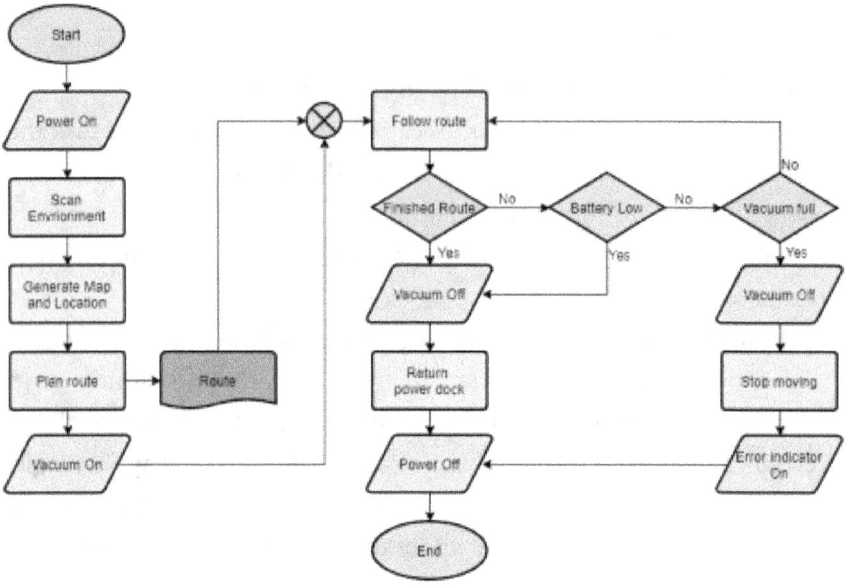

An algorithm that exists only in your head is fragile. It can be misunderstood, misremembered, or implemented incorrectly. One of the most important skills in computer science is therefore not just designing algorithms, but **expressing them clearly so that others and computers can follow them precisely**. This chapter focuses on two foundational communication tools: pseudocode and flowcharts. Together, they bridge the gap between human thinking and executable programs.

As you will see, expressing an algorithm is not about choosing a single "correct" format. Instead, it is about flexibility. The same idea can be represented in words, diagrams, structured pseudocode, or full programming languages, and each representation highlights different aspects of the logic. Skilled problem solvers move comfortably between these forms.

Why Representation Matters

When beginners first encounter algorithms, they often believe that the final goal is code. In practice, jumping directly to code is one of the most common sources of confusion and error. Code is unforgiving, and small mistakes in syntax can hide deeper problems in logic.

Pseudocode and flowcharts act as **thinking tools**. They allow you to focus on *what* the algorithm does before worrying about *how* a specific programming language requires it to be written. They also serve as shared languages between team members who may use different programming tools but need to agree on behavior.

In professional settings, algorithms are frequently discussed, reviewed, and revised in pseudocode or diagrams long before any code is written.

Pseudocode: Writing Algorithms for Humans

Pseudocode is a structured, informal way of describing an algorithm. It looks similar to programming code but avoids strict syntax rules. Its primary goal is clarity, not execution.

Key Characteristics of Good Pseudocode

Good pseudocode uses clear, consistent keywords, such as START, END, IF, ELSE, WHILE, and FOR. It uses indentation to show structure and avoids unnecessary detail. Variable names are descriptive rather than short or cryptic, and each step represents a meaningful action.

These conventions matter because pseudocode is often read by people with different technical backgrounds. Consistency reduces misunderstanding, and clarity reduces errors when translating the logic into real code.

Example 1: Making Tea

Before dealing with numbers or data, consider a familiar daily activity.

Plain-language description

You boil water, place a tea bag in a cup, pour the hot water, wait a few minutes, and then drink the tea.

Pseudocode representation

```
START
Fill kettle with water
Heat water until boiling
Place tea bag in cup
Pour hot water into cup
Wait for 3 minutes
Remove tea bag
END
```

This example shows that pseudocode does not need to be complex to be precise. Each step is clear, ordered, and unambiguous.

Flowcharts: Visualizing Control Flow

Flowcharts represent algorithms visually using standardized shapes. Ovals typically represent start and end points, rectangles represent actions, and diamonds represent decisions. Arrows show the direction of flow.

Flowcharts are especially helpful for understanding branching logic and loops, because the visual structure makes paths through the algorithm immediately visible.

They are widely used in education, system design, and documentation.

For the tea-making algorithm, a flowchart would show a linear sequence of steps, with a possible decision point for checking whether the water has boiled.

Example 2: Finding the Maximum Number in a List

Now consider a slightly more technical problem: finding the largest number in a list.

Pseudocode

```
START
Set max to first number in list
FOR each remaining number in list
IF number is greater than max
```

```
Set max to number
END FOR
Output max
END
```

This pseudocode introduces looping and decision-making while remaining readable.

Flowchart perspective

A flowchart for this algorithm would include a loop that repeatedly compares the current number with the stored maximum. The decision diamond visually reinforces the idea that only one of two paths is taken at each comparison.

Seeing the Same Algorithm in Multiple Forms

One of the most important lessons in this chapter is that **representation does not change the algorithm itself**. The logic remains the same whether it is expressed in words, pseudocode, a flowchart, or a programming language.

Translation to Python

```
numbers = [3, 7, 2, 9, 5]
max_value = numbers[0]
for num in numbers[1:]:
if num > max_value:
max_value = num
print(max_value)
```

Translation to Java

```
int[] numbers = {3, 7, 2, 9, 5};
int maxValue = numbers[0];
for (int i = 1; i < numbers.length; i++) {
if (numbers[i] > maxValue) {
maxValue = numbers[i];
}
}
System.out.println(maxValue);
```

Although Python and Java look different, both implementations follow the exact same algorithm described in the pseudocode. This demonstrates why expressing ideas clearly before coding is so powerful.

Example 3: Decision-Based Algorithm (Pass or Fail)

Consider an algorithm that determines whether a student passes an exam.

Pseudocode

```
START
Input score
IF score is greater than or equal to 50
Output "Pass"
ELSE
Output "Fail"
END IF
END
```

This example highlights how decision structures are expressed consistently across representations. A flowchart would make the branching immediately visible, while pseudocode emphasizes readability.

Common Pitfall: Mixing Pseudocode with Real Code

A frequent beginner mistake is writing pseudocode that depends heavily on the syntax of a specific programming language. This defeats the purpose of pseudocode, which should remain language-independent. The goal is to describe logic clearly, not to compile or run the algorithm.

Example 4: Repetition with a Condition

Imagine an algorithm that keeps asking for a password until the correct one is entered.

This example is particularly effective when shown side by side in pseudocode and a flowchart, because the looping behavior is easier to grasp visually while the pseudocode clarifies the condition being checked.

Exercises: Converting Between Representations

To strengthen your understanding, practice moving between forms.

Take a flowchart that describes checking whether a number is even or odd and write its pseudocode. Then translate that pseudocode into Python or Java. Next, take a short piece of code and rewrite it as clean pseudocode, focusing only on logic and ignoring syntax details.

These exercises train you to see algorithms as abstract ideas rather than fixed blocks of code.

Appendix: Pseudocode Style Guide

Pseudocode should always begin and end clearly, use consistent keywords, and rely on indentation rather than punctuation to show structure. Conditions should read like natural language, and loops should state their purpose clearly. Variables should be named for meaning rather than convenience.

Following a style guide is not about being rigid; it is about making your thinking visible and accessible to others.

Reflection

Expressing algorithms is an act of communication. Whether you are explaining an idea to a teammate, documenting a system, or preparing to write code, clear representations reduce errors and increase confidence. As problems grow more complex, the ability to shift smoothly between pseudocode, flowcharts, and code becomes not just helpful, but essential.

4. Analyzing Algorithmic Efficiency

Up to this point, we have focused on designing and expressing algorithms clearly. However, an algorithm that works correctly is not always an algorithm that works *well.* When problems are small, inefficiency often goes unnoticed. As problems grow, the difference between a good algorithm and a poor one can become dramatic, sometimes even catastrophic. This chapter is about understanding *why* efficiency matters and how computer scientists' reason about it in a systematic way.

Imagine sorting a list of 1,000 items. Now imagine sorting 1,000,000 items using the same method. If the algorithm becomes one thousand times slower, that may still be acceptable. If it becomes one million times slower, it may be unusable. Algorithmic efficiency is about anticipating this growth before systems fail, users leave, or costs spiral out of control.

Why Efficiency Matters: A Thought Experiment

Consider a simple task: finding a specific name in a list. If the list contains ten names, you could check them one by one without concern. If the list contains one thousand names, the same approach still feels reasonable. Now imagine a list containing one million names. Checking each name one by one suddenly feels slow and frustrating.

This difference is not about hardware speed alone. It is about how the number of steps required by an algorithm grows as the input size grows. A computer that can perform billions of operations per second will still struggle if an algorithm requires trillions of operations. Efficiency, therefore, is not a luxury; it is a necessity for scalability.

This is why algorithm designers ask a specific question: *What happens when the input size increases dramatically?*

Counting Operations: Building Intuition

Before introducing formal notation, it helps to start with something concrete. Suppose you are given a list of numbers and asked to find the largest one.

If the list has five numbers, you might compare each number once, resulting in four comparisons. If the list has ten numbers, you need nine comparisons. If the list has one thousand numbers, you need nine hundred and ninety-nine comparisons. The pattern is clear: the number of operations grows in direct proportion to the number of items.

This simple act of counting operations manually builds intuition. You begin to see that what matters is not the exact time in seconds, but the *rate of growth* as the problem size increases.

Library Search as an Analogy

Imagine searching for a book in a library. One approach is to start at the first shelf and check every book until you find the one you want. This method works, but it becomes slower as the library grows. Another approach is to use an index or catalog, allowing you to jump directly to the correct section and then narrow down your search.

The first approach resembles a **linear search**, where time grows steadily with the number of books. The second approach resembles a **logarithmic search**, where each step dramatically reduces the remaining search space. Even without mathematics, it is easy to see which approach scales better as the library expands.

Introducing Big-O Notation

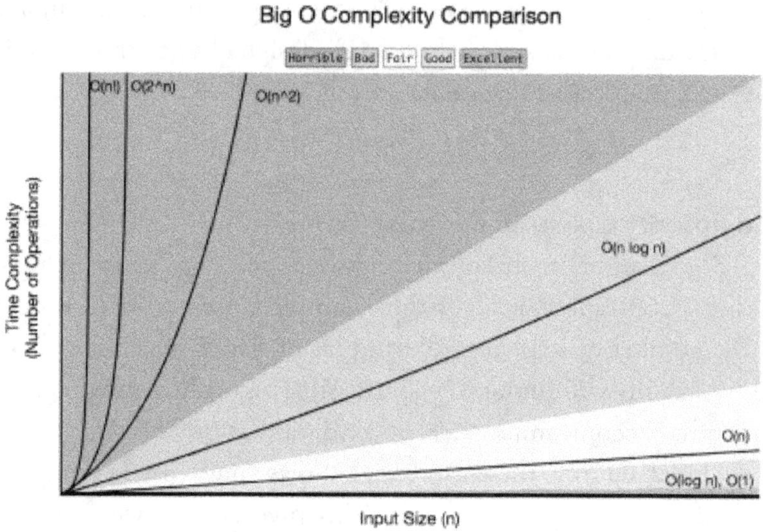

Big-O notation is a way of describing how an algorithm's running time grows relative to input size. It does not measure exact time, because exact time depends on hardware and implementation details. Instead, it captures the dominant growth pattern.

When we say an algorithm runs in *O(n)* time, we mean that its running time grows linearly with the number of inputs. When we say it runs in *O(log n)* time, we mean that each step reduces the problem size significantly, leading to much slower growth. When we say $O(n^2)$, we mean that the work grows rapidly as input size increases.

Big-O notation gives us a shared language for comparing algorithms, even when they are written in different programming languages or run on different machines.

Seeing Growth Visually

Graphs are especially helpful for understanding complexity. A linear growth curve rises steadily. A logarithmic curve rises quickly at first and then flattens. A quadratic curve starts gently and then rises sharply. When these curves are placed side by side, the long-term consequences of design choices become obvious.

An algorithm that seems "fast enough" for small inputs may become unusable at scale, while a well-designed algorithm continues to perform smoothly even as data grows.

Complexity Classes in Everyday Terms

Some common complexity classes appear repeatedly in algorithm design. Constant time algorithms complete their work in roughly the same number of steps regardless of input size. Linear time algorithms grow steadily with input. Quadratic time algorithms grow much faster and often become impractical beyond modest input sizes.

Understanding these categories allows you to predict performance before writing or running code. This predictive power is one of the most valuable skills in computer science.

Complexity at a Glance

Think of complexity classes as growth personalities. Constant time algorithms are calm and predictable. Logarithmic algorithms are clever and efficient. Linear algorithms are straightforward and honest. Quadratic algorithms are dangerous at scale, while exponential algorithms are usually avoided except for very small problems.

Keeping this mental reference close at hand helps you make better design decisions instinctively.

Comparing Algorithms with Real-World Runtimes

Consider two algorithms processing one million items. A linear algorithm might complete in a fraction of a second on modern hardware. A quadratic algorithm might take hours or days. This difference is not theoretical; it determines whether systems feel responsive or broken.

Tables that compare input size to estimated runtime make this contrast tangible. They show that efficiency is not about small optimizations, but about choosing the right approach from the beginning.

The Instagram Case Study: Why Scalability Is Everything

When you open **Instagram**, you expect your feed to load almost instantly, even though millions of new photos and videos are uploaded every day. Early versions of social media feeds could rely on simple chronological ordering. As user bases exploded, this approach became impractical.

Instagram's systems must rank content, filter spam, personalize recommendations, and do so for hundreds of millions of users simultaneously. Algorithms that worked at small scale had to be replaced with ones that scale efficiently. Even small inefficiencies, when multiplied by millions of users, translate into enormous costs and delays.

This case study makes scalability tangible. Algorithmic efficiency is not an academic exercise; it directly affects user experience, infrastructure cost, and system reliability.

Common Pitfall: Focusing on Small Inputs

Beginners often test algorithms only with small examples, leading to false confidence. An algorithm that feels fast with ten items may collapse under ten million. Efficiency analysis forces you to think beyond immediate tests and consider future growth.

Gradually Introducing the Math

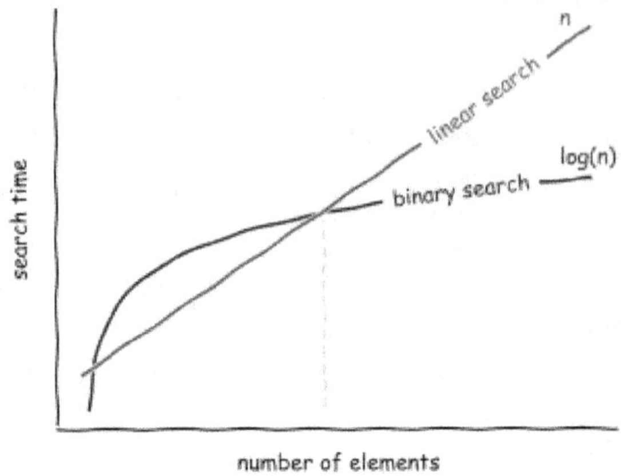

At its core, complexity analysis relies on simplified mathematical reasoning. We ignore constant factors and focus on dominant terms because they determine long-term behavior. This abstraction may feel strange at first, but it reflects practical reality. When input sizes grow large, dominant terms overwhelm all others.

Understanding this idea prepares you for more formal analysis later, without requiring advanced mathematics at this stage.

Reflection: Thinking at Scale

Analyzing algorithmic efficiency changes how you see problems. You stop asking only whether a solution works and begin asking whether it will continue to work as the world grows larger. This shift in perspective is one of the defining characteristics of computational thinking.

5. Brute Force and Exhaustive Search

In the world of algorithms, brute force often has a bad reputation. It is sometimes described as naïve, inefficient, or unsophisticated. Yet this reputation is only half deserved. Brute force is the most **honest** approach to problem solving: it tries every possibility in a straightforward, transparent way and guarantees correctness when given enough time. In many real situations, this simplicity is not a weakness but a strength.

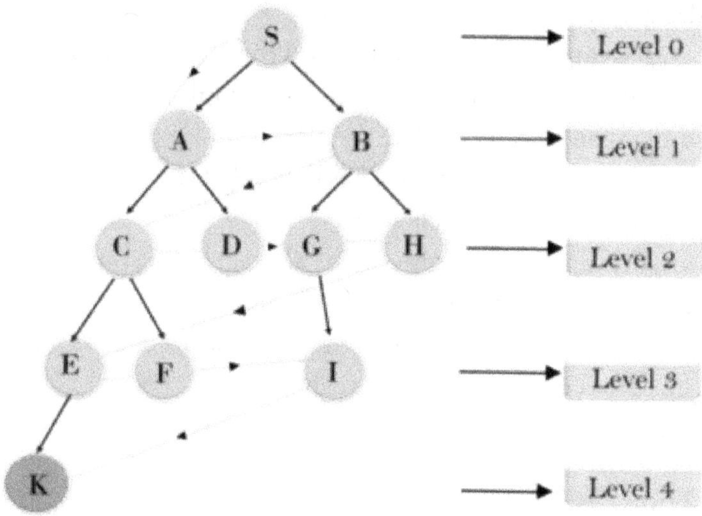

This chapter reframes brute force as a legitimate and sometimes optimal strategy. You will learn when brute force is the right choice, when it becomes dangerous, and how professionals optimize brute-force approaches to reduce unnecessary work. We will ground these ideas in familiar algorithms such as linear search and bubble sort, and we will examine password cracking as a security case study that reveals both the power and the risks of exhaustive search.

What Brute Force Really Means

A brute-force algorithm solves a problem by checking **all possible candidates** until it finds the correct one or exhausts the search space. It does not rely on clever shortcuts or assumptions about structure. Instead, it relies on completeness. If a solution exists within the defined space, brute force will find it.

This approach has three defining characteristics. First, it is simple to design and understand. Second, it is easy to implement correctly. Third, its performance depends directly on the size of the search space. When that space is small, brute force can be surprisingly effective. When it is large, brute force can quickly become impractical.

Understanding this trade-off is essential for responsible algorithm design.

Linear Search: The Simplest Honest Algorithm

Linear search is the most direct example of brute force. Given a list of items and a target value, the algorithm checks each item one by one until it finds a match or reaches the end of the list.

How Linear Search Works

The algorithm begins at the first element and compares it to the target. If the element matches, the search stops. If not, the algorithm moves to the next element and repeats the process. This continues until the item is found or the list is exhausted.

Python Implementation

```
def linear_search(items, target):
"""
Searches for target in the list items.
Returns the index if found, otherwise returns -1.
"""
for index in range(len(items)):
if items[index] == target:
return index
```

```
return -1
```

This implementation is easy to read, easy to test, and very hard to get wrong. For small lists or unsorted data, linear search is often the best possible choice.

Step-by-Step Execution Trace

Imagine searching for the number 7 in the list [2, 4, 6, 7, 9].

The algorithm compares 2 with 7, then 4 with 7, then 6 with 7, and finally 7 with 7. The search stops immediately once the match is found. This trace makes it clear why linear search performs well when the target appears early, and why performance degrades when the target is near the end or absent.

Bubble Sort: Brute Force Sorting

Bubble sort is another classic brute-force algorithm. It sorts a list by repeatedly stepping through it, comparing adjacent elements, and swapping them if they are in the wrong order. This process continues until the list is sorted.

Why Bubble Sort Matters

Bubble sort is rarely used in production systems, but it is invaluable for learning. Its logic is transparent, its behavior is predictable, and its inefficiency is easy to observe. These qualities make it an ideal teaching tool for understanding brute force.

Python Implementation

```
def bubble_sort(items):
"""

Sorts the list items in ascending order using bubble sort.
"""

n = len(items)
for i in range(n):
for j in range(0, n - i - 1):
if items[j] > items[j + 1]:
items[j], items[j + 1] = items[j + 1], items[j]
return items
```

This algorithm checks all adjacent pairs repeatedly, even when much of the list is already sorted. That redundancy is precisely what makes bubble sort inefficient at scale.

Optimizing Brute Force Without Abandoning It

Brute force does not mean careless force. Small optimizations can significantly reduce unnecessary work while preserving simplicity.

In bubble sort, for example, we can stop early if no swaps occur during a pass. This does not change the fundamental approach, but it improves performance for partially sorted lists.

Optimized Bubble Sort

```
def optimized_bubble_sort(items):
"""
Bubble sort with early stopping if the list is already sorted.
"""
n = len(items)
for i in range(n):
swapped = False
for j in range(0, n - i - 1):
if items[j] > items[j + 1]:
items[j], items[j + 1] = items[j + 1], items[j]
swapped = True
if not swapped:
break
return items
```

This version respects the brute-force philosophy while eliminating wasted passes.

Password Cracking: Exhaustive Search in the Real World

Password cracking provides a powerful and sobering example of brute force. In a brute-force password attack, an attacker systematically tries every possible password combination until the correct one is found.

From an algorithmic perspective, this is exhaustive search at its purest. From a security perspective, it reveals why brute force must be taken seriously.

Short passwords with limited character sets are vulnerable because the search space is small. Longer passwords with diverse characters dramatically increase the number of possibilities, making brute-force attacks computationally infeasible.

This is why modern security practices emphasize password length, complexity, rate limiting, and hashing. They are all designed to make brute force too expensive to succeed.

Security Implications and Ethical Responsibility

Understanding brute force is essential for defense as well as offense. Security professionals must think like attackers in order to design systems that resist exhaustive search. At the same time, ethical responsibility requires that these techniques be studied for protection, not misuse.

This chapter treats password cracking as an educational case study, not a how-to guide, reinforcing the idea that algorithmic knowledge carries real-world responsibility.

When to Use Brute Force

Brute force is often the right choice when the input size is small, when correctness is more important than speed, when no better algorithm is known, or when the problem will only be solved once or infrequently. It is also an excellent baseline for testing and validating more advanced algorithms.

However, brute force should be avoided when input sizes grow rapidly, when performance is critical, or when the search space is unbounded. Recognizing this boundary is a key professional skill.

Limitations You Must Respect

The primary limitation of brute force is scalability. Exhaustive search grows quickly as problem size increases, and this growth can overwhelm even powerful machines. Respecting these limits prevents wasted effort and system failures.

Brute force also encourages a mindset that may overlook problem structure. While simplicity is valuable, ignoring patterns can lead to missed opportunities for dramatic improvement.

Reflection: Honest Work, Honest Limits

Brute-force algorithms teach an important lesson. They remind us that clarity, correctness, and simplicity are virtues, not embarrassments. At the same time, they teach humility by revealing how quickly naïve approaches reach their limits.

As you move forward, you will encounter more sophisticated strategies that outperform brute force by exploiting structure and insight. Those strategies are best understood when you first appreciate the honest baseline that brute force provides.

6. Divide and Conquer

Some algorithms impress through sheer cleverness, while others impress through clarity and balance. Divide and conquer belongs firmly in the second category. It is elegant because it mirrors how humans naturally approach difficult problems: instead of wrestling with everything at once, we split the problem into smaller pieces, solve those pieces confidently, and then combine the results.

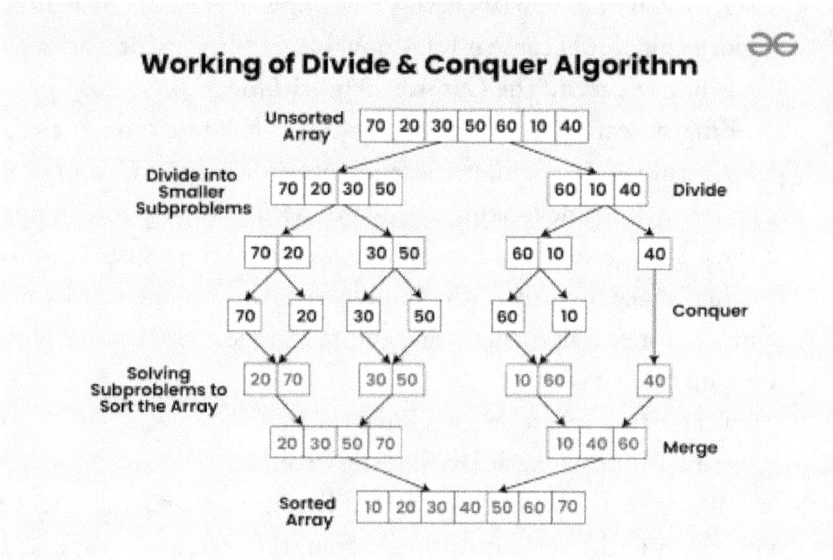

In this chapter, you will learn divide and conquer as a disciplined way of thinking rather than a collection of tricks. We will begin with binary search, an algorithm that feels almost magical the first time you see how much work it saves. From there, we will carefully build up to merge sort, using detailed visual breakdowns to show how complex behavior emerges from simple rules. Along the way, recursion will be introduced gently and deliberately, with enough repetition and explanation to allow it to sink in naturally rather than feel intimidating.

The Core Idea Behind Divide and Conquer

At its heart, divide and conquer follows a simple pattern. First, divide the problem into smaller subproblems that resemble the original problem. Second, conquer those subproblems by solving them, often using the same approach recursively. Third, combine the solutions to form the final answer.

What makes this approach powerful is that each division reduces the size of the problem significantly. Instead of making slow progress through a large task, divide and conquer shrinks the challenge rapidly until what remains is easy to solve directly.

This structure appears across computer science, mathematics, and engineering, not because it is fashionable, but because it works.

Binary Search: The Gateway Algorithm

Binary search is often the first divide-and-conquer algorithm people truly understand, because its intuition is grounded in everyday experience. Imagine looking up a word in a dictionary. You do not start at the first page and read forward one word at a time. Instead, you open the dictionary roughly in the middle, see whether the word you want comes before or after that page, and then repeat the process with half the remaining pages.

That instinctive strategy is binary search.

How Binary Search Divides the Problem

Binary search works on a sorted list. It compares the target value with the middle element. If they match, the search is complete. If the target is smaller, the algorithm discards the right half of the list. If the target is larger, it discards the left half. Each comparison eliminates half of the remaining possibilities.

This repeated halving is the essence of divide and conquer, and it explains why binary search is dramatically faster than linear search for large datasets.

Binary Search and Recursion

Binary search can be implemented iteratively or recursively. The recursive version makes the divide-and-conquer structure especially clear.

There is a **base case**, where the search range becomes empty or the element is found. There is also a **recursive case**, where the algorithm calls itself on a smaller half of the list. Each recursive call solves a smaller version of the same problem.

Understanding this pattern is crucial, because it reappears in every divide-and-conquer algorithm you will encounter.

Visualizing Binary Search with a Recursion Tree

A recursion tree for binary search shows a single path descending through smaller and smaller ranges. Each level of the tree represents one comparison, and the height of the tree reflects how many steps are required. Because the range is halved each time, the tree grows slowly, which explains the algorithm's efficiency.

Seeing this structure visually often makes the algorithm feel less abstract and more intuitive.

Recursion: Removing the Mystery

Recursion often intimidates beginners because it feels like a function calling itself endlessly. In reality, recursion is controlled repetition with clear stopping conditions. Every recursive algorithm must answer two questions clearly: when does it stop, and how does it make progress toward that stopping point?

A useful mental model is to imagine delegation. Each function call delegates a smaller version of the problem to another instance of itself, trusting that instance to do its job correctly. The base case is the moment when no further delegation is needed.

Taking time to internalize this model pays dividends throughout algorithm design.

Merge Sort: Divide and Conquer at Scale

Merge sort takes the divide-and-conquer idea and applies it to sorting. Instead of comparing elements one by one in place, merge sort splits the list into halves repeatedly until each sub list contains a single element. At that point, the algorithm begins merging these tiny lists back together in sorted order.

What makes merge sort elegant is that sorting two already sorted lists is straightforward and efficient. The algorithm does not try to sort everything at once; it builds order gradually through combination.

Step-by-Step Breakdown of Merge Sort

The dividing phase of merge sort continues until the problem becomes trivial. A list with one element is already sorted, so no work is needed. The conquering phase then begins, merging pairs of sorted lists into larger sorted lists.

Visual split-merge diagrams are especially valuable here.

They show the list being broken apart symmetrically and then reassembled, reinforcing the idea that the algorithm's power comes from structure rather than brute force.

Merge Sort and Recursion Trees

A recursion tree for merge sort looks very different from the one for binary search. Instead of a single path, the tree branches widely, representing multiple recursive calls at each level. Each level of the tree processes the entire dataset, but the number of levels grows slowly.

This structure explains why merge sort is efficient even for very large inputs and why its performance remains predictable regardless of input order.

Introducing the Master Theorem Gently

The Master Theorem is a mathematical tool used to analyze divide-and-conquer algorithms. At this stage, it is best understood as a shortcut rather than a burden. Instead of manually analyzing recursion trees every time, the Master

Theorem provides patterns that tell you how an algorithm's running time grows.

You do not need to memorize formulas immediately. What matters is recognizing that divide-and-conquer algorithms often follow predictable performance patterns because of their structured splitting and combining.

Database Sorting: A Real-World Case Study

Large databases rely heavily on divide-and-conquer sorting algorithms to manage massive volumes of data efficiently. Systems such as **Oracle Database must sort records for queries, indexing, and reporting, often dealing with datasets far larger than available memory.

Merge sort and its variants are particularly valuable in this context because they can be adapted for external storage, where data is read and written in chunks. The same principles you learn here scale up to systems that serve millions of users and process terabytes of information daily.

This case study demonstrates that divide and conquer is not just elegant in theory, but indispensable in practice.

Recursion Checklist

When designing a recursive divide-and-conquer algorithm, it helps to slow down and verify a few essentials. You should be able to clearly identify the base case, ensure that each recursive call reduces the problem size, confirm that all subproblems are eventually solved, and verify that the combination step is correct and efficient.

Using such a checklist prevents subtle bugs and infinite recursion, especially when problems become more complex.

Allowing Time for Understanding

Divide and conquer often feels deceptively simple once it clicks, but reaching that moment takes patience. It is normal to revisit examples multiple times and to trace through recursive calls slowly. This investment of time builds intuition that will support far more advanced algorithms later.

Rather than rushing, allow the patterns to become familiar. With practice, you will begin to recognize divide-and-conquer opportunities instinctively.

Reflection: The Beauty of Structured Thinking

Divide and conquer shows that elegance in algorithms comes from thoughtful structure rather than clever shortcuts. By trusting recursion, respecting base cases, and combining solutions carefully, you can solve problems that initially seem overwhelming.

7. Greedy Algorithms

Not every problem requires deep planning or exhaustive exploration. In many situations, making a locally good decision at each step leads to a globally optimal outcome. Greedy algorithms are built on this idea of *good enough decision-making*, where the algorithm commits to what looks best right now and never looks back. This approach can feel risky, yet when applied to the right problems, greedy algorithms are remarkably powerful and efficient.

This chapter explores greedy algorithms with both optimism and caution. You will learn why greedy strategies sometimes work beautifully, why they sometimes fail dramatically, and how to tell the difference before committing to them. We will begin with the classic activity selection problem, move into proof techniques that justify greedy choices, and then examine counterexamples that reveal greedy's limitations. The chapter culminates in a case study of Huffman coding, where greedy decision-making enables real-world data compression at massive scale.

What Makes an Algorithm Greedy

A greedy algorithm builds a solution step by step, always choosing the option that seems best according to a specific criterion at that moment. Once a choice is made, it is never reconsidered. This lack of backtracking is what gives greedy algorithms their efficiency and simplicity, but it is also what makes them dangerous when applied carelessly.

Greedy algorithms are appealing because they are usually easy to understand, fast to execute, and memory efficient. They often feel intuitive, mirroring how humans make decisions under time pressure. However, intuition alone is not enough. A greedy algorithm is only correct when the problem structure guarantees that locally optimal choices lead to a globally optimal solution.

The Activity Selection Problem

The activity selection problem provides an ideal introduction to greedy thinking. You are given a set of activities, each with a start time and a finish time, and the goal is to select the maximum number of non-overlapping activities that can be performed by a single person.

At first glance, the problem invites many possible strategies. You might choose the shortest activities, the ones that start earliest, or the ones that finish earliest. Only one of these strategies leads to an optimal solution.

The correct greedy strategy is to always select the activity that finishes earliest among those compatible with the already selected activities. Once that activity is chosen, all overlapping activities are discarded, and the process repeats.

Why the Greedy Choice Works Here

The success of this strategy is not accidental. Choosing the activity that finishes earliest leaves as much remaining time as possible for future activities. Any solution that begins with a later-finishing activity can be transformed into one that begins with the earliest-finishing activity without reducing the total number of activities selected.

This reasoning leads us to an important concept: **proof by exchange argument**. We show that if an optimal solution does not include the greedy choice, we can exchange part of that solution with the greedy choice and still obtain an optimal solution. This demonstrates that the greedy choice is safe.

Although informal, this type of proof is rigorous enough to justify the algorithm's correctness and is widely used in algorithm design.

Visualizing Greedy Decisions

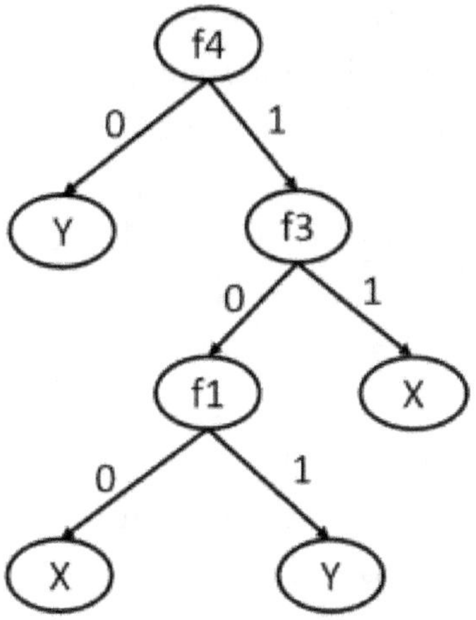

Tree 1

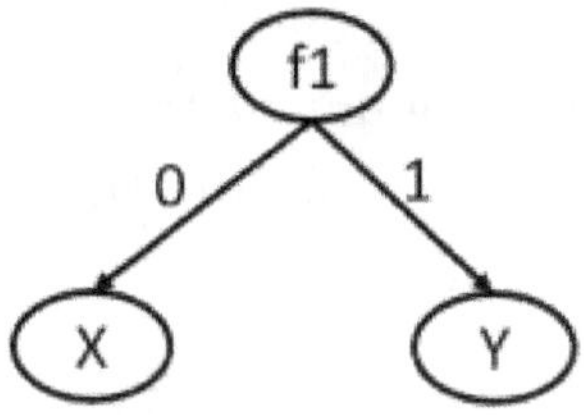

Tree 2

Decision diagrams make greedy behavior easier to understand. In the activity selection problem, a timeline visualization shows how choosing an early-finishing activity opens up space for additional choices later. Each greedy decision prunes the future decision tree aggressively, which explains both the algorithm's speed and its reliance on correctness of the initial criterion.

Seeing these choices visually reinforces the idea that greedy algorithms succeed when the problem's structure aligns with the greedy rule.

The Greedy Choice Property and Optimal Substructure

Two properties are essential for greedy algorithms to work. The first is the **greedy choice property**, which guarantees that a locally optimal choice can be part of a globally optimal solution. The second is **optimal substructure**, meaning that once a greedy choice is made, the remaining problem is still an optimal instance of the original problem.

If either of these properties fails, greedy algorithms become unreliable. Learning to recognize these properties is far more important than memorizing specific greedy algorithms.

When Greedy Fails: A Cautionary Example

Consider a coin change problem where you must make a certain amount using the fewest coins possible. In some currency systems, choosing the largest coin available at each step works perfectly. In others, it fails.

For example, with coin denominations of 1, 3, and 4, a greedy approach for making 6 would choose 4, then 1, then 1, resulting in three coins. The optimal solution uses two coins: 3 and 3. The greedy algorithm makes a locally sensible choice that leads to a globally suboptimal outcome.

This example highlights why greedy algorithms cannot be trusted without proof. A strategy that works beautifully in one context may fail silently in another.

Another Failure Case: Shortest Path Misconceptions

It is tempting to believe that always choosing the shortest immediate edge in a graph will lead to the shortest overall path. This intuition fails in many cases. A locally short edge may lead into a region of the graph that forces long detours later.

This misconception is valuable because it shows that greedy thinking must be supported by structural guarantees, not just intuition. Some shortest path algorithms are greedy, but they succeed only because they maintain additional invariants that preserve correctness.

Huffman Coding: Greedy Algorithms at Their Best

Huffman coding provides one of the most celebrated successes of greedy algorithms. The problem is to design a binary encoding scheme for characters such that the total size of the encoded data is minimized, given known character frequencies.

The greedy strategy repeatedly combines the two least frequent symbols into a single node, building a binary tree from the bottom up. This approach feels almost too simple, yet it produces an optimal prefix code.

The correctness of Huffman coding can be justified using an exchange argument that shows the two least frequent symbols can always be placed at the deepest level of the tree in an optimal solution. By committing to this choice early, the algorithm reduces the problem size while preserving optimality.

Real-World Impact of Huffman Coding

Huffman coding is used in many compression formats, including image, audio, and document storage. Every time data is compressed efficiently, greedy algorithms are quietly at work. This case study demonstrates that greedy strategies are not merely theoretical curiosities, but practical tools with enormous real-world impact.

Balancing Power with Caution

Greedy algorithms are seductive because of their simplicity and speed. When they work, they often outperform more complex approaches. When they fail, they can produce plausible-looking but incorrect solutions that are difficult to detect.

Professional algorithm designers therefore approach greedy methods with both enthusiasm and skepticism. They ask not only whether a greedy rule seems reasonable, but whether it can be justified rigorously.

The Greedy Checklist

Before committing to a greedy solution, it is wise to pause and ask a few key questions. Can you clearly define a greedy choice? Does making that choice leave a subproblem that is structurally identical to the original problem? Can you argue, using an exchange argument, that an optimal solution exists that includes the greedy choice? If these questions cannot be answered convincingly, greedy is probably the wrong tool.

Reflection: Trust, but Verify

Greedy algorithms teach an important lesson about decision-making under constraints. Acting decisively can be powerful, but only when the structure of the problem supports that decisiveness. By learning both the strengths and weaknesses of greedy strategies, you develop judgment rather than habit.

8. Dynamic Programming

For many students, dynamic programming is the moment where algorithms begin to feel truly challenging. The ideas are subtle, the examples are layered, and the solutions are rarely obvious at first glance. This reaction is completely normal. Dynamic programming is not difficult because it is mysterious or mathematical, but because it asks you to change *how* you think about solving problems.

Dynamic programming, often abbreviated as DP, can be understood as **smart recursion with memory**. It takes the elegance of recursive problem solving and strengthens it by remembering past work, ensuring that no effort is wasted. This chapter moves slowly and deliberately, building intuition before formal technique, and returning repeatedly to visual explanations so that understanding has time to settle.

Why Dynamic Programming Exists

To appreciate dynamic programming, you must first feel the pain it is designed to solve. Consider a problem that can be broken into overlapping subproblems. If you solve those subproblems repeatedly without remembering the results, your algorithm may waste enormous amounts of time doing the same work again and again.

Dynamic programming exists to eliminate this waste. It preserves the clarity of recursive thinking while introducing a disciplined way to store and reuse intermediate results. When applied correctly, DP transforms algorithms that are impractical into ones that scale gracefully.

Fibonacci Numbers: The Classic Motivation

The Fibonacci sequence is often the first example used to introduce dynamic programming, not because it is complex, but because it exposes inefficiency clearly.

A naïve recursive Fibonacci algorithm defines the nth Fibonacci number as the sum of the two previous ones. This definition is mathematically elegant and easy to express in code. Unfortunately, it is computationally disastrous.

When you draw the recursion tree for this algorithm, you see the same Fibonacci values being recomputed over and over again. The tree grows explosively, even for modest input sizes. This repeated work is the core problem that dynamic programming addresses.

Memorization: Remembering What You Already Know

Memorization is the first dynamic programming technique most people learn. The idea is simple: whenever you compute the result of a subproblem, you store it in a table. Before computing a result, you check whether it has already been computed.

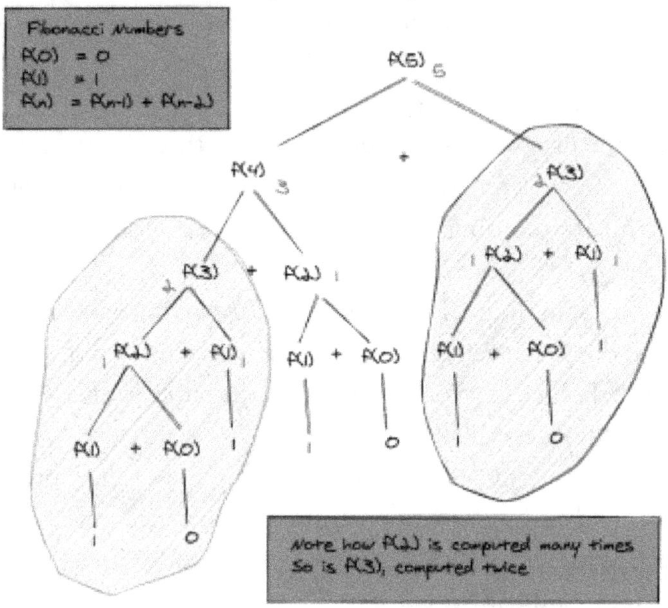

This small change has a dramatic effect. The recursion tree collapses, because each subproblem is solved only once. What was once exponential time becomes linear time.

Visually, a recursion tree with memorization looks sparse and controlled, with repeated branches replaced by quick table lookups. This visual contrast helps explain why memorization is so powerful.

From Top-Down to Bottom-Up Thinking

While memorization improves recursive solutions, it still relies on recursion. Tabulation, the second major DP technique, takes a different approach. Instead of starting with the full problem and breaking it down, tabulation starts with the smallest subproblems and builds up to the full solution.

This bottom-up perspective can feel unfamiliar at first. However, it often leads to clearer, more efficient implementations. Dynamic programming tables make dependencies explicit and remove the need for recursion entirely.

Understanding both memorization and tabulation is important, because some problems are more naturally expressed one way than the other.

Understanding DP Tables

A dynamic programming table is a structured way of storing solutions to subproblems. Each cell represents a partial solution, and the table is filled according to a carefully defined order that respects dependencies.

The key to designing a DP table lies in answering three questions clearly. What does each cell represent? How is each cell computed from previously filled cells? In what order should the table be filled to ensure all required values are available?

Visualizing these tables is essential. Seeing how values propagate across rows and columns turns abstract recurrence relations into concrete processes.

Example: Climbing Stairs

Consider the problem of counting the number of distinct ways to climb a staircase where you can take either one or two steps at a time. This problem has a recursive structure very similar to Fibonacci, and it suffers from the same repeated-work issue when implemented naïvely.

Using dynamic programming, you define a table where each entry represents the number of ways to reach a particular step. The table is filled sequentially, with each value depending only on the previous two. This example reinforces the idea that DP is not about clever tricks, but about disciplined bookkeeping.

The Spell Checker Case Study

Modern spell checkers rely heavily on dynamic programming to compare words efficiently. One of the core tasks is computing the *edit distance* between two strings, which measures how many insertions, deletions, or substitutions are required to transform one word into another.

Applications such as **Google Search** use this concept to suggest corrections when a user misspells a query. The algorithm constructs a two-dimensional DP table where each cell represents the edit distance between prefixes of the two words.

This table-based approach ensures that each comparison is computed once and reused. Without dynamic programming, spell checking at scale would be far too slow to be practical.

Visualizing Edit Distance with DP Tables

The edit distance table is a powerful teaching tool. Each row corresponds to a prefix of the first word, and each column corresponds to a prefix of the second. The value in each cell is derived from neighboring cells, reflecting insertion, deletion, and substitution operations.

Watching this table fill in gradually makes it clear how local decisions combine into a global solution. It also demonstrates why DP problems often involve grids or matrices.

Recognizing Dynamic Programming Problems

One of the hardest skills to develop is recognizing when dynamic programming is appropriate. Not every problem requires DP, and forcing it where it does not belong leads to unnecessary complexity.

Dynamic programming is a strong candidate when a problem exhibits overlapping subproblems and optimal substructure. Overlapping subproblems mean that the same smaller problems appear repeatedly. Optimal substructure means that an optimal solution to the problem can be built from optimal solutions to its subproblems.

Learning to spot these patterns comes with practice and repeated exposure.

The DP Recognition Pattern

When faced with a new problem, ask yourself whether the problem can be broken into smaller versions of itself. Consider whether solving those smaller problems independently and reusing their results would save work. Look for a natural way to index subproblems, often by size, position, or prefix length.

If you can define a recurrence relation and a storage structure for results, you are likely dealing with a dynamic programming problem.

Another Example: The Knapsack Problem

The knapsack problem asks how to choose items with given weights and values to maximize total value without exceeding a weight limit. Greedy strategies fail for this problem in general, making it an ideal candidate for dynamic programming.

The DP solution builds a table where rows represent items and columns represent weight limits. Each cell captures the best achievable value under those constraints. This example highlights how DP systematically explores trade-offs rather than committing early.

Why Dynamic Programming Feels Hard

Dynamic programming requires holding multiple perspectives at once. You must think about the full problem, the subproblems, the recurrence relation, and the storage structure simultaneously. This cognitive load is what makes DP challenging, not the mathematics.

The key is patience. By slowing down, drawing tables, and tracing small examples, the logic becomes clearer. Mastery comes from repetition, not speed.

Practice Problems with Graduated Difficulty

Begin with problems that closely resemble Fibonacci and climbing stairs. Progress to grid-based path counting problems, then to string comparison tasks like longest common subsequence. Each step adds a layer of complexity while reinforcing the same core ideas.

For each problem, practice identifying subproblems, defining the DP table, and deciding on a filling order. These habits matter more than memorizing solutions.

Reflection: Learning to Remember

Dynamic programming teaches an important lesson beyond algorithms. It rewards careful thought, patience, and respect for previous work. By remembering what you have already solved, you avoid frustration and inefficiency.

This mindset applies beyond computing, encouraging deliberate progress rather than repeated struggle. In the next chapter, we will turn to graph algorithms, where dynamic programming ideas often reappear in new and surprising forms.

9. Backtracking

Some problems do not have a single clear path forward. Instead, they resemble a maze of possibilities, where each decision opens new options while closing others. Backtracking is the algorithmic technique designed for exactly this situation. It is **systematic exploration with intelligence**, a method that tries possibilities one by one, abandons them as soon as they prove invalid, and retreats gracefully to try alternatives.

At first glance, backtracking may look like brute force in disguise. In reality, it is brute force refined by structure, logic, and early rejection of bad paths. This chapter treats backtracking as a disciplined search strategy, one that is especially well suited to puzzles, games, and constraint-based problems. Through visual examples such as the N-Queens puzzle and Sudoku, you will see how backtracking turns overwhelming search spaces into manageable explorations.

From Brute Force to Intelligent Search

Brute force explores every possible solution without discrimination. Backtracking explores the same space, but **with awareness**. The key difference lies in *pruning*: the ability to stop exploring a path as soon as it violates the problem's constraints.

Backtracking works incrementally. It builds a partial solution step by step, checking at each stage whether the current state is still valid. If a violation is detected, the algorithm immediately backtracks, undoing the last decision and trying a different option. This early rejection prevents vast amounts of unnecessary work.

Understanding this distinction helps clarify why backtracking is powerful without being reckless.

State Space and Search Trees

To understand backtracking clearly, it helps to think in terms of a **state space**. Each state represents a partial solution, and transitions between states represent choices. When visualized, this space forms a tree, often called a *state space tree*.

The root of the tree represents the empty solution. Each level represents a new decision. Leaves represent complete solutions or dead ends. Backtracking performs a depth-first traversal of this tree, exploring one branch fully before moving on to the next.

Visualizing this tree makes the algorithm's behavior far more intuitive, especially when pruning removes entire subtrees at once.

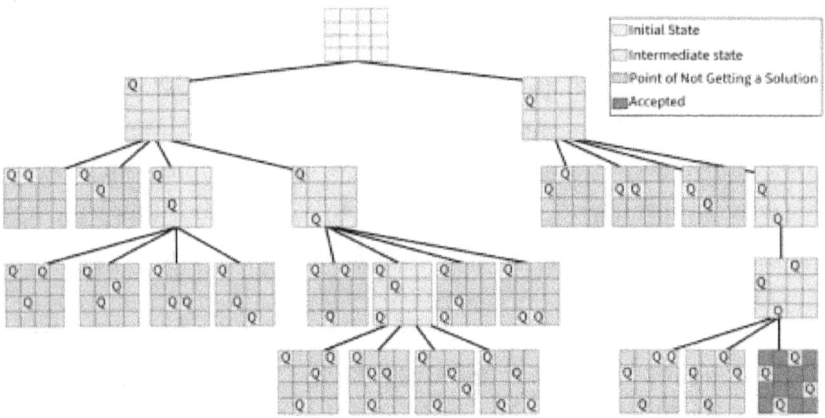

The N-Queens Problem: A Perfect Introduction

The N-Queens problem asks whether it is possible to place N queens on an N×N chessboard so that no two queens attack each other. Queens attack along rows, columns, and diagonals, which makes the constraints easy to state but surprisingly hard to satisfy.

This problem is ideal for learning backtracking because it is highly visual and its constraints are immediately understandable. You place queens one row at a time, ensuring that each new queen does not conflict with the ones already placed.

Backtracking Through N-Queens

The algorithm begins by placing a queen in the first row, trying each column in turn. For each placement, it checks whether the position is safe relative to previously placed queens. If it is safe, the algorithm moves to the next row. If not, that position is rejected immediately.

When the algorithm reaches a row where no safe column exists, it backtracks to the previous row and tries a different column. This continues until either a full solution is found or all possibilities are exhausted.

Search tree diagrams are especially helpful here. They show how large portions of the tree are pruned early, long before reaching the deepest levels.

Pruning: The Heart of Backtracking

Pruning is what makes backtracking efficient. The moment a partial solution violates a constraint, the algorithm stops exploring that branch entirely. There is no need to see how bad a solution becomes if it is already invalid.

In N-Queens, pruning occurs when two queens share a column or diagonal. In other problems, pruning conditions may be more subtle, but the principle is the same: reject early, save time.

The effectiveness of backtracking depends heavily on how early and how cheaply these constraint checks can be performed.

Sudoku: Backtracking in Action

Sudoku is one of the most familiar examples of backtracking in everyday life. The puzzle requires filling a grid with numbers so that each row, column, and subgrid contains all digits exactly once.

A backtracking Sudoku solver fills in empty cells one by one. For each cell, it tries all possible digits that satisfy the current constraints. If a choice later leads to a contradiction, the algorithm backtracks and tries a different digit.

What makes Sudoku engaging is that humans often use intuition and heuristics, while the algorithm relies purely on systematic exploration and constraint checking. Watching a solver work reveals the raw power of backtracking.

Constraint Satisfaction Problems

Backtracking is the foundation of a broader class of problems known as **constraint satisfaction problems**. In these problems, the goal is to assign values to variables while satisfying a set of constraints.

Examples include scheduling, resource allocation, puzzle solving, and configuration tasks. The common structure is that partial assignments can be checked for validity before they are complete, making them ideal candidates for backtracking.

Thinking in terms of variables, domains, and constraints provides a reusable framework that applies far beyond puzzles.

How Backtracking Relates to Brute Force

Backtracking does not eliminate brute force; it refines it. In the worst case, backtracking may still explore an exponential number of possibilities. The difference is that backtracking avoids obviously bad paths early, often making the difference between feasible and infeasible solutions.

This perspective is important. Backtracking is not magic, and it does not guarantee efficiency. Its strength lies in exploiting structure and constraints to reduce unnecessary exploration.

The Backtracking Template

Most backtracking algorithms follow the same conceptual structure. You choose a variable, iterate over possible values, check whether the choice is valid, recurse to the next variable if it is, and undo the choice if it leads to failure.

Seeing this template repeatedly helps build confidence. While the problems may look different on the surface, the underlying logic remains remarkably consistent.

Interactive Challenge: Try It Yourself

Imagine a 4×4 chessboard and attempt to solve the 4-Queens problem by hand. Place queens' row by row and note when you are forced to backtrack. Drawing the board and marking conflicts makes the process concrete and reinforces the idea of pruning.

Similarly, try solving a small Sudoku puzzle by deliberately filling in one cell at a time and backing up when contradictions arise. These hands-on exercises make the algorithm feel tangible rather than abstract.

When Backtracking Is the Right Tool

Backtracking shines when problems have clear constraints, when partial solutions can be checked cheaply, and when the solution space is large but structured. It is especially effective for puzzles, combinatorial generation, and decision problems where solutions must satisfy strict rules.

It is less suitable when constraints are weak or when partial validity cannot be determined early. Recognizing this distinction helps you choose backtracking wisely.

Reflection: Exploring Without Panic

Backtracking teaches a valuable mindset. It encourages exploration without fear of mistakes, because mistakes are expected and reversible. By committing temporarily and retreating, when necessary, the algorithm mirrors a calm and methodical approach to uncertainty.

10. Searching Algorithms

Searching is one of the most fundamental operations in computing. Almost every system you interact with search engines, contact lists, file explorers, databases spend a significant amount of its time answering a single question: *is the thing I am looking for here, and if so, where is it?* The difference between a slow system and a fast one is often determined not by hardware, but by how searching is performed.

This chapter presents searching algorithms as a progression from simple to sophisticated. We begin with linear search, which establishes a clear baseline. We then move to binary search, where structure unlocks dramatic performance gains. Finally, we explore hashing, which introduces the remarkable possibility of constant-time search. Along the way, we will repeatedly search the same dataset using different methods so that the performance trade-offs become tangible rather than abstract.

Why Search Algorithms Deserve Special Attention

At small scales, almost any search method feels fast enough. Searching ten names in a list takes virtually no time, regardless of how it is done. At large scales, however, the choice of search algorithm becomes critical. Searching millions or billions of records efficiently is one of the core challenges of modern computing.

Search algorithms are also pedagogically important because they make algorithmic efficiency visible. You can often *feel* the difference between linear, logarithmic, and constant-time behavior even with modest input sizes. This makes searching an ideal domain for building performance intuition.

Linear Search: Establishing the Baseline

Linear search is the simplest possible searching strategy. Given a collection of items, the algorithm checks each item one by one until it finds the target or reaches the end of the collection. No assumptions are made about ordering or structure.

This approach is honest and reliable. It works on any dataset and is trivial to implement correctly. For very small datasets or one-time searches, linear search is often the right choice because its simplicity outweighs its inefficiency.

From a performance perspective, linear search scales directly with the size of the dataset. Doubling the number of items roughly doubles the number of comparisons. This linear growth makes it a useful baseline against which more advanced methods can be measured.

Visualizing Linear Search

A linear search visualization shows a pointer moving steadily through a list from left to right. Each comparison is independent, and no information gained early in the search helps later steps. This lack of progress acceleration explains why linear search becomes slow as datasets grow.

Despite its limitations, linear search remains relevant. It performs well on unsorted data, works with streams, and requires no preprocessing.

Binary Search: Power from Structure

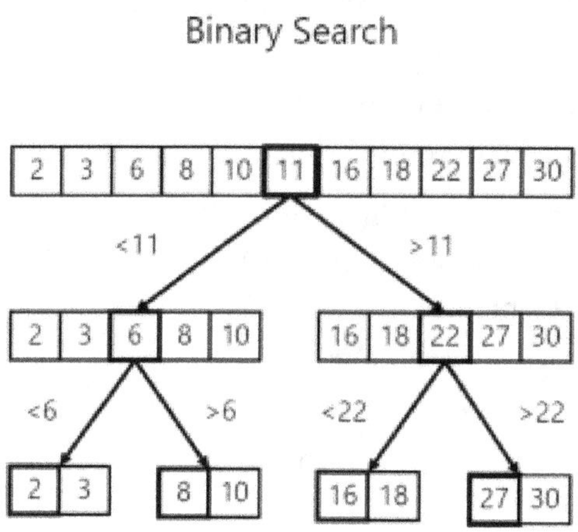

Binary search represents a dramatic leap in efficiency, but it comes with a crucial requirement: the data must be sorted. This single structural assumption allows the algorithm to discard half of the remaining search space at every step.

Binary search compares the target with the middle element of the dataset. If the target is smaller, the algorithm continues searching in the left half. If it is larger, the search continues in the right half. This halving repeats until the target is found or the search space is empty.

The performance improvement is striking. Even for millions of items, binary search completes in a small number of steps. This logarithmic growth is one of the most important ideas in algorithm design.

Seeing Logarithmic Growth in Action

Search visualizations for binary search highlight its efficiency immediately. Instead of scanning element by element, the algorithm jumps across the dataset, narrowing the search range aggressively. Performance graphs comparing linear and binary search show lines that diverge rapidly as input size increases, making the advantage unmistakable.

Binary search teaches an essential lesson: *structure enables speed.* Without sorted data, binary search is impossible. With it, searching becomes dramatically more efficient.

Hashing: The Promise of Constant-Time Search

Hashing takes a different approach entirely. Instead of repeatedly narrowing a search range, hashing attempts to compute the location of an item directly using a hash function. Ideally, this allows searches to complete in constant time, written as O (1).

A hash table stores key–value pairs. The hash function transforms a key into an index, where the corresponding value is stored. When searching, the same

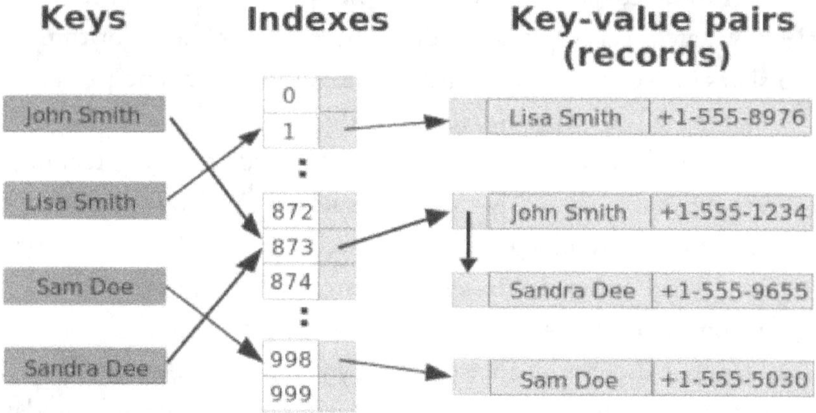

hash function is applied to the key, and the algorithm looks directly at the computed location.

This approach feels almost magical when it works well. Searching no longer depends on the number of stored items, at least in the average case.

Understanding the Cost Behind O(1)

The promise of constant-time search comes with important caveats. Hash functions can produce collisions, where different keys map to the same index. Handling collisions introduces extra work and complexity. Memory usage is also higher, and performance depends on maintaining a good balance between table size and number of stored items.

These trade-offs explain why hashing is powerful but not universally applicable. It excels when fast lookups are required and memory is available, but it is not always the right choice.

Comparing Search Algorithms on the Same Dataset

To make these differences concrete, imagine searching a dataset of one million records. A linear search may require hundreds of thousands of comparisons on average. A binary search requires only around twenty comparisons. A hash-based search typically requires just one or two operations.

Performance tables comparing these approaches make the contrast clear. What looks like a small design decision at the algorithm level translates into orders-of-magnitude differences in runtime.

Database Indexing: Search at Scale

Modern databases rely heavily on advanced searching techniques to retrieve data efficiently. Systems such as **MySQL** use indexing structures that resemble tree-based searches rather than simple scans. These indexes allow databases to locate records quickly even when tables contain millions or billions of rows.

Database indexes balance the ideas you have already seen. They rely on structure, like binary search, while also supporting dynamic updates. Without efficient search algorithms, databases would grind to a halt under real-world workloads.

This case study connects theory to practice, showing that searching is not an academic exercise, but a foundation of modern information systems.

Search Algorithm Selector

Choosing the right search algorithm depends on several factors. If the data is small or unsorted and searched infrequently, linear search may be sufficient. If the data is sorted and relatively static, binary search offers excellent performance with minimal overhead. If extremely fast lookups are required and memory usage is acceptable, hashing becomes attractive.

Thinking in terms of these trade-offs leads to better system design than blindly applying the most sophisticated method available.

Strengths and Weaknesses Side by Side

Linear search is flexible and simple but slow at scale. Binary search is fast but depends on sorted data. Hashing is extremely fast on average but introduces complexity and memory costs. No single approach dominates in all situations.

Comparative charts that summarize time complexity, space requirements, and data assumptions help reinforce this balanced view.

Reflection: Searching as a Design Choice

Searching algorithms highlight a recurring theme in computer science: performance emerges from structure and informed trade-offs. There is no universally best algorithm, only algorithms that are well matched to their context.

As you move forward, remember that searching rarely exists in isolation. It is often combined with sorting, indexing, and data organization strategies. In the next chapter, we will explore sorting algorithms in depth, completing the core toolkit that underpins efficient data processing.

11. Sorting Algorithms

Sorting is one of the most studied and refined problems in computer science. At first glance, it appears simple: arrange items in order. Yet beneath this simplicity lies a rich landscape of ideas, trade-offs, and design philosophies. Sorting algorithms differ not only in speed, but in memory usage, predictability, adaptability, and even personality. Understanding these differences helps you choose the right tool rather than merely the fastest one on paper.

This chapter surveys sorting algorithms comprehensively while maintaining focus on what truly matters. We group algorithms by strategy, visualize how each behaves, and repeatedly sort the same array to make their differences concrete. Along the way, we examine why real systems rely on hybrid approaches such as TimSort, and why concepts like stability matter more often than beginners expect.

Why Sorting Deserves Deep Attention

Sorting is rarely an end in itself. It is a gateway operation that enables faster searching, easier comparison, efficient grouping, and meaningful presentation of data. Many algorithms assume sorted input, and many systems spend a significant portion of their time sorting intermediate results.

Because sorting sits at the intersection of theory and practice, it provides an ideal setting for comparing algorithmic strategies. You can see how abstract ideas such as divide and conquer or brute force translate directly into observable behavior.

Two Families of Sorting Algorithms

Sorting algorithms fall naturally into two broad families: **comparison-based** and **non-comparison-based** sorts.

Comparison-based algorithms determine order by comparing pairs of elements. Because they rely on comparisons, they are subject to fundamental performance limits. Non-comparison-based algorithms, by contrast, exploit assumptions about the data, such as limited ranges or digit structure, to bypass these limits.

This distinction shapes both performance and applicability, making it a useful organizing principle for understanding the sorting landscape.

Bubble Sort: Simplicity Above All

Bubble sort is often the first sorting algorithm people encounter. It repeatedly steps through the list, compares adjacent elements, and swaps them if they are in the wrong order. Larger elements gradually "bubble" to the end of the list.

Bubble sort's personality is gentle and transparent. Every step is easy to follow, and its behavior is predictable. This makes it excellent for teaching, debugging, and visualization. At the same time, its inefficiency becomes painfully obvious as input size grows.

When sorting the same array with bubble sort, you can almost feel the algorithm working harder than necessary, revisiting the same comparisons again and again.

Insertion Sort: Order Emerging Gradually

Insertion sort builds a sorted portion of the array one element at a time. Each new element is inserted into its correct position among those already sorted. This mirrors how people often sort playing cards by hand.

Its personality is patient and adaptive. Insertion sort performs very well on nearly sorted data, where only small adjustments are needed. This makes it far more useful in practice than its worst-case analysis alone would suggest.

Watching insertion sort operate reveals a smooth, incremental refinement of order rather than chaotic swapping.

Selection Sort: Methodical but Unforgiving

Selection sort repeatedly selects the smallest remaining element and places it in the correct position. Its behavior is methodical and consistent, performing the same number of comparisons regardless of input order.

This consistency makes selection sort easy to analyze, but also inefficient. It ignores opportunities to adapt to partially sorted data, which limits its practical value despite its conceptual clarity.

Merge Sort: Reliability Through Structure

Merge sort embodies the divide-and-conquer philosophy. It splits the array into halves, sorts each half recursively, and then merges the sorted halves into a single sorted array.

Its personality is calm and reliable. Merge sort's performance is predictable and stable across all inputs. It does not degrade on already sorted or adversarial data, which makes it highly trustworthy.

Visual split-and-merge diagrams reveal the algorithm's symmetry and explain why its performance scales so well.

Quicksort: Speed with Risk

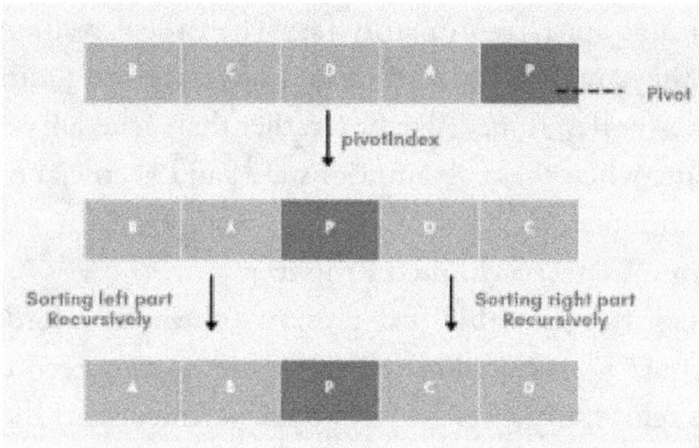

Quicksort is often the fastest sorting algorithm in practice, yet it comes with caveats. It selects a pivot element, partitions the array around that pivot, and recursively sorts the partitions.

Its personality is bold and energetic. When pivot selection is good, quicksort is astonishingly fast. When it is poor, performance can degrade significantly. This sensitivity makes quicksort both powerful and dangerous.

Visualizing quicksort's partitions helps explain why its average-case performance is excellent and why careful implementation choices matter so much.

Sorting the Same Array, Different Behaviors

Sorting the same unsorted array with different algorithms highlights their personalities clearly. Bubble sort makes many small, repetitive moves. Insertion sort slides elements smoothly into place. Merge sort reorganizes the array in large structural steps. Quicksort rapidly carves the array into smaller regions.

These visual differences reinforce that algorithms are not just abstract formulas, but processes with distinct rhythms and costs.

Non-Comparison Sorting: Breaking the Rules

Non-comparison-based algorithms such as counting sort and radix sort achieve linear-time performance by exploiting assumptions about the data. Instead of comparing elements directly, they distribute elements into buckets or process digits systematically.

These algorithms are extraordinarily fast when their assumptions hold. However, they are limited in scope and often require additional memory. Their power lies in specialization rather than generality.

Understanding when these assumptions are valid is crucial before applying such techniques.

Stability: An Often-Overlooked Property

A sorting algorithm is **stable** if it preserves the relative order of elements with equal keys. Stability matters when sorting records by multiple fields, such as sorting employees by department and then by name.

Merge sort and insertion sort are stable by nature, while quicksort and selection sort are not unless modified. This distinction has practical consequences in real systems, where data often carries layered meaning.

Stability is not about speed, but about correctness in context.

TimSort: Sorting in the Real World

Most production systems do not rely on a single "pure" sorting algorithm. Instead, they use hybrids engineered to perform well across diverse scenarios. TimSort, used in Python and maintained by the **Python Software Foundation**, is a prime example.

TimSort combines ideas from merge sort and insertion sort. It detects existing order in the data and exploits it aggressively, achieving excellent performance on real-world inputs that often contain patterns.

This case study reveals an important lesson: algorithm engineering is about adapting theory to reality, not blindly applying textbook solutions.

Performance and Use-Case Comparisons

Detailed comparison tables make the trade-offs explicit. Some algorithms prioritize simplicity, others prioritize speed, and others prioritize predictability. Memory usage, stability, and adaptability all influence which algorithm is appropriate in a given situation.

These comparisons reinforce the idea that there is no universally best sorting algorithm, only algorithms that are well matched to specific needs.

Sorting Algorithm Cheat Sheet

A compact summary of sorting algorithms, their strategies, time complexities, stability, and typical use cases serves as a valuable reference. Such a cheat sheet is not meant for memorization, but for informed decision-making when designing systems.

Reflection: Order as a Design Choice

Sorting algorithms illustrate how different design philosophies can solve the same problem in radically different ways. By learning their personalities and trade-offs, you move beyond rote knowledge and toward judgment.

12. Graph Algorithms

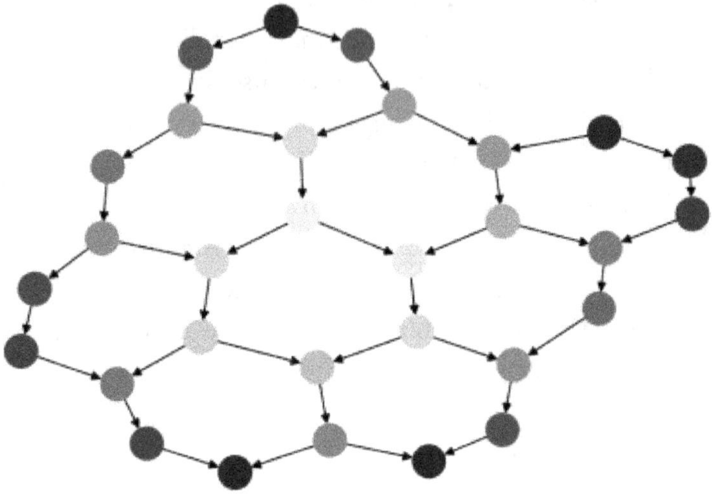

Graphs are everywhere, even when we do not call them by that name. Every time you scroll through a social network, navigate city streets, browse recommendations, or analyze communication patterns, you are interacting with graph-shaped data. Graph algorithms matter because so many real-world problems are fundamentally about **relationships rather than sequences**. Where arrays and lists focus on order, graphs focus on connection.

This chapter builds intuition before technique. Rather than starting with formal definitions, we begin with familiar networks and gradually uncover the structure that makes graph algorithms both powerful and necessary. Breadth-first search and depth-first search form the backbone of graph thinking, and we will study them carefully before progressing to shortest path algorithms. Throughout the chapter, real-world applications anchor abstract ideas, culminating in a friend-suggestion case study that makes graphs feel personal and relevant.

Thinking in Networks Instead of Lines

Most of the algorithms you have seen so far operate on linear structures. Lists, arrays, and tables all impose a clear order. Graphs abandon this simplicity. In a graph, each element can connect to many others, and there may be multiple paths between any two points.

This shift in perspective is crucial. When you think in graphs, you stop asking "what comes next?" and start asking "what is connected to what?" This change opens the door to modeling complex systems such as social relationships, transportation networks, computer networks, and biological systems.

Graphs capture not just data, but *structure*, and that structure often carries the most important information.

Social Networks as Graphs

A social network is one of the most intuitive examples of a graph. Each person is a node, and each friendship is an edge. Some people are highly connected, while others have only a few connections. Groups form naturally, and information spreads along these connections.

Platforms such as **Facebook** rely heavily on graph algorithms to understand and manage these relationships. Friend suggestions, content ranking, community detection, and even security analysis all depend on efficient graph processing.

By starting with social networks, graphs become less abstract and more human.

Basic Graph Concepts Without Heavy Formalism

At a high level, a graph consists of vertices (also called nodes) and edges that connect them. Edges may be directed or undirected, weighted or unweighted. These distinctions matter because they influence which algorithms are appropriate.

A friendship graph is typically undirected, because the relationship is mutual. A follower graph is directed, because one person may follow another without reciprocity. A road network is often weighted, with distances or travel times assigned to edges.

Understanding these variations prepares you to choose the right traversal and path-finding strategies later.

Why Traversal Is Fundamental

Before solving complex graph problems, you must answer a simpler question: how do you systematically visit every node in a graph? Graph traversal is the foundation upon which nearly all graph algorithms are built.

Traversal algorithms must handle cycles, disconnected components, and irregular structures. Unlike arrays, graphs do not guarantee that moving forward will eventually reach every element. Traversal provides that guarantee.

Breadth-First Search: Exploring Level by Level

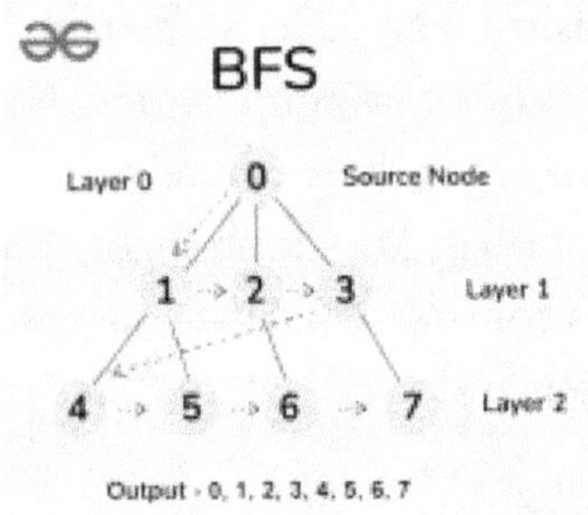

Breadth-first search, commonly abbreviated as BFS, explores a graph one layer at a time. Starting from a source node, it visits all immediate neighbors before moving on to neighbors of neighbors.

BFS feels natural in social contexts. If you think about degrees of separation, BFS is exactly the algorithm that finds all friends, then friends of friends, then friends of friends of friends. This layered exploration makes BFS especially useful for shortest-path problems in unweighted graphs.

Visualization is particularly helpful here. BFS traversal diagrams show concentric waves expanding outward from the source, reinforcing the idea of level-by-level discovery.

Depth-First Search: Exploring Paths Fully

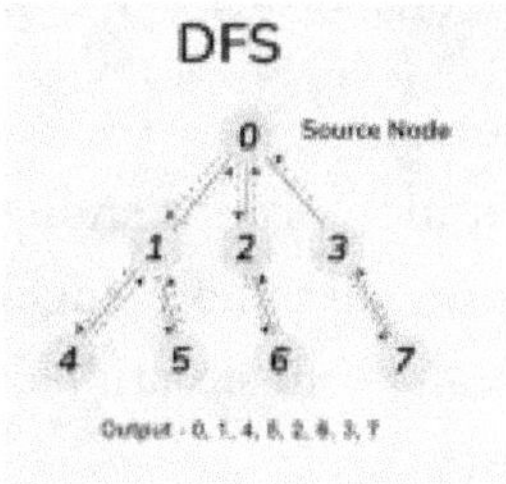

Depth-first search, or DFS, takes a very different approach. Instead of expanding outward evenly, it follows one path as far as it can before backtracking and trying another.

DFS feels exploratory and curious. It is well suited for tasks such as maze solving, cycle detection, and connectivity analysis. DFS reveals the structure of the graph deeply, uncovering long chains of connection before moving sideways.

Traversal animations help clarify the contrast between BFS and DFS. Where BFS feels broad and methodical, DFS feels narrow and adventurous.

BFS and DFS as Foundational Tools

Although BFS and DFS are simple, they are remarkably versatile. Many advanced graph algorithms use them as building blocks. Understanding their behavior, strengths, and limitations is far more important than memorizing their code.

BFS excels at finding shortest paths in unweighted graphs and at analyzing layers of connectivity. DFS excels at exploring structure, detecting cycles, and organizing graphs hierarchically.

Together, they form the grammar of graph algorithms.

From Traversal to Shortest Paths

Once traversal is understood, the next natural question is how to find efficient paths through a graph. Shortest path algorithms answer questions such as: What is the fastest route between two cities? How can data travel with minimal delay? Which connections matter most?

In unweighted graphs, BFS already provides shortest paths. In weighted graphs, the problem becomes more complex, requiring more sophisticated techniques.

Weighted Graphs and Practical Complexity

When edges carry weights, traversal order alone is not enough. A path with fewer edges may be slower than one with more edges but lower total weight. This complexity mirrors real-world situations, such as choosing between highways and local roads.

Shortest path algorithms must balance exploration with careful cost accounting. This is where algorithms like Dijkstra's algorithm enter the picture, building on traversal ideas while adding prioritization.

Friend Suggestions: A Graph Case Study

Friend suggestion systems rely on graph algorithms to identify meaningful connections. A common heuristic is "friends of friends," which naturally aligns with BFS traversal. However, real systems go further, weighing mutual connections, interaction history, and shared communities.

This case study highlights how abstract graph ideas translate into personal experiences. The suggestion that appears on your screen is the result of graph exploration, scoring, and filtering performed at massive scale.

Understanding this process demystifies recommendation systems and reveals the algorithmic thinking behind them.

Graphs Beyond Social Networks

Graphs model transportation systems, communication networks, dependency graphs in software, and knowledge graphs in search engines. In each case, nodes represent entities, and edges represent relationships or interactions.

The same traversal and path-finding algorithms apply across these domains, demonstrating the universality of graph thinking. Learning graph algorithms therefore equips you with tools that transfer easily between disciplines.

Balancing Theory and Practice

Graph theory provides formal definitions and proofs, while graph algorithms focus on computation and application. This chapter emphasizes the practical side, without losing sight of the underlying structure.

The goal is not to memorize formulas, but to develop intuition about how information flows through networks and how algorithms can harness that flow efficiently.

Graph Algorithm Reference

A quick reference guide summarizing BFS, DFS, and shortest path approaches serves as a mental map for navigating graph problems. Such a guide reinforces relationships between algorithms and helps you choose the right tool quickly.

Reflection: Seeing the World as Connections

Graph algorithms change how you perceive systems. You begin to see networks instead of isolated elements, paths instead of sequences, and influence instead of order. This relational mindset is essential for understanding modern computing systems.

13. Tree Algorithms

Trees are the most natural way to represent hierarchy. Wherever information is organized into levels where some elements depend on, contain, or refine others a tree structure quietly appears. File systems, organizational charts, XML documents, programming language syntax, and database indexes all rely on trees because trees mirror how humans' structure complex ideas.

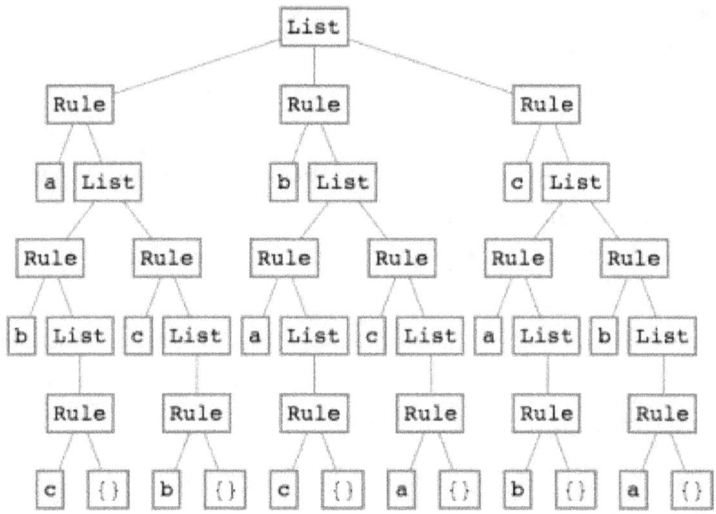

This chapter presents trees as **fundamental structural tools**, not merely as data structures to memorize. We begin with simple binary trees and binary search trees to build intuition. From there, we confront the central challenge of tree-based algorithms: imbalance. Self-balancing trees such as AVL and Red-Black trees demonstrate how engineering tradeoffs shape real systems. Throughout the chapter, careful visual walkthroughs ensure that operations such as insertion, deletion, and rotation feel mechanical rather than mysterious.

Why Trees Matter

Unlike arrays or graphs, trees impose a clear hierarchy. Every node except the root has a parent, and each subtree represents a meaningful substructure of the whole. This organization allows trees to support efficient searching, insertion, deletion, and ordered traversal—often all at once.

Trees are especially powerful because they strike a balance between rigidity and flexibility. They are more structured than graphs, which simplifies reasoning, yet more expressive than linear lists, which limits performance. This balance explains why trees appear so frequently in both theoretical and practical systems.

From Hierarchy to Data Structure

At an abstract level, a tree consists of nodes connected by edges, with one distinguished root node. Each node may have zero or more children. When we impose constraints on how many children a node may have, or how values are arranged, different kinds of trees emerge.

A family tree, for example, is not constrained to two children, while a binary tree is. These constraints are not arbitrary; they shape what operations are efficient and how algorithms behave.

Binary Trees: The Structural Baseline

A binary tree restricts each node to at most two children, traditionally called the left child and the right child. This simple constraint makes binary trees easy to visualize and reason about.

Binary trees are not necessarily ordered. Their value lies in structure, not in search efficiency. Traversals such as preorder, in order, and post order illustrate how the same tree can be processed in multiple meaningful ways, depending on context.

Understanding traversal order is essential, because it reappears in searching, sorting, expression evaluation, and file system operations.

Binary Search Trees: Structure with Order

Binary search trees, or BSTs, add an ordering rule to the binary tree structure. For every node, all values in the left subtree are smaller, and all values in the right subtree are larger. This invariant is what enables efficient searching.

Searching a BST resembles binary search on an array, but with dynamic structure. At each node, you decide whether to go left or right based on a comparison. This decision process repeats recursively until the value is found or a leaf is reached.

When balanced, a BST offers logarithmic-time performance for search, insertion, and deletion.

BST Operations with Visual Walkthroughs

Insertion into a BST follows the same logic as search. You traverse the tree until you find an appropriate empty position, then insert the new node there. Deletion is more subtle, especially when removing nodes with two children, because the ordering property must be preserved.

Visual step-by-step diagrams are invaluable here. They show how local changes ripple through the structure and why certain cases require careful handling. Without such visuals, BST deletion often feels arbitrary; with them, it becomes systematic.

The Hidden Problem: Tree Imbalance

Binary search trees promise efficient operations, but that promise depends on balance. If values are inserted in sorted order, the tree degenerates into a linked list. In that case, operations degrade from logarithmic time to linear time.

This vulnerability is not a theoretical edge case. In real systems, input patterns are rarely random. Relying on luck for balance is unacceptable in production environments.

Recognizing this problem motivates the development of self-balancing trees.

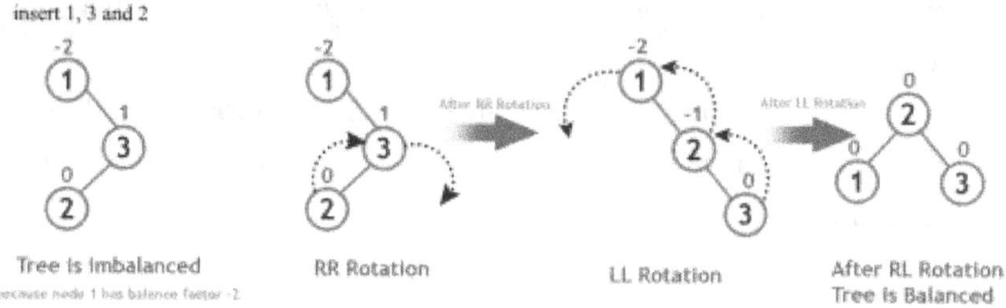

AVL Trees: Strict Balance, Predictable Performance

AVL trees enforce a strict balance condition. For every node, the height difference between its left and right subtrees is tightly bounded. Whenever this condition is violated, the tree performs **rotations** to restore balance.

Rotations are local structural transformations that preserve the BST ordering while redistributing height. Although they look complex at first, rotation diagrams reveal a consistent mechanical process.

AVL trees prioritize search speed and predictability, sometimes at the cost of more frequent rebalancing during insertions and deletions.

Understanding Rotations Visually

Rotation animations are essential for understanding self-balancing trees. They show that rotations do not randomly rearrange nodes, but instead reorganize them in a precise, rule-driven way.

By tracing rotations step by step, you see that balance is restored without violating ordering constraints. This insight transforms rotations from intimidating procedures into reliable tools.

Red-Black Trees: Engineering Tradeoffs

Red-Black trees relax AVL's strict balance requirements in favor of looser constraints enforced through node coloring rules. These rules guarantee that the tree remains approximately balanced, ensuring logarithmic performance without excessive rebalancing.

This design reflects an engineering compromise. Red-Black trees perform fewer rotations and handle insertions and deletions more smoothly, making them well suited for systems with heavy update workloads.

Many standard libraries and systems choose Red-Black trees precisely because of this balance between performance and maintenance cost.

Trees in the Real World: File Systems

File systems are one of the most tangible examples of tree structures. Directories contain files and subdirectories, forming a rooted hierarchy that mirrors a tree perfectly.

Operating systems such as **Linux** represent file paths as tree traversals. Commands that list directories, search for files, or compute disk usage all rely on tree algorithms operating over this structure.

This case study reinforces that trees are not abstract constructs, but practical tools that organize everyday digital life.

Tree Traversal in Practice

Traversal algorithms determine how trees are processed. Preorder traversal is useful for copying trees or serializing structure. In order traversal of a BST produces sorted output. Post order traversal supports safe deletion of nodes.

Understanding these traversals deepens your ability to reason about recursive algorithms, because traversal order directly reflects recursion structure.

Pointer and Reference Discipline

Implementing tree algorithms requires careful handling of pointers or references. Each insertion, deletion, or rotation involves updating multiple links consistently. Small mistakes can corrupt the structure silently.

This is why tree algorithms demand discipline and patience. Careful step-by-step reasoning, supported by diagrams, prevents subtle errors and builds confidence.

Tree Type Selection Guide

Choosing the right tree depends on workload characteristics. Simple BSTs may suffice for small or controlled datasets. AVL trees are ideal when search speed is critical. Red-Black trees excel in environments with frequent updates. Understanding these tradeoffs allows you to choose structures intentionally rather than by habit.

Reflection: Thinking in Layers

Tree algorithms cultivate hierarchical thinking. They encourage you to reason locally while respecting global structure, and to design algorithms that scale gracefully as systems grow.

A	B	A	B	D	A	B	A	C	D	A	B	A	B	C	A	B	A	B

A	B	A	B	C	A	B	A	B

Failure function:

j	0	1	2	3	4	5	6	7	8
P[j]	A	B	A	B	C	A	B	A	B
f(j)	0	0	1	2	0	1	2	3	4

14. String and Pattern Matching Algorithms

Strings are the raw material of the digital world. Every search query, email, DNA sequence, log file, source code repository, and social media post ultimately reduces to sequences of characters that must be stored, compared, analyzed, and searched. While numbers often dominate early algorithm discussions, text processing is where algorithms meet human language, biological data, and large-scale information retrieval. String and pattern matching algorithms exist to answer a deceptively simple question: *where does this pattern occur within this text?*

This chapter treats string algorithms as foundational tools for modern computing. We begin with the most direct approach to pattern matching, not because it is efficient, but because it establishes a clear baseline. From there, we move to more sophisticated algorithms that demonstrate how careful preprocessing and pattern awareness can eliminate vast amounts of unnecessary work. Throughout the chapter, visual explanations ground abstract ideas, and real-world applications show why these algorithms matter at scale.

Why String-Matching Matters So Much

Searching text is not an isolated task. It underpins search engines, spell checkers, intrusion detection systems, plagiarism detection tools,

DNA analysis pipelines, and countless other applications. Unlike numeric problems, string matching often operates on massive datasets where patterns are short but texts are enormous.

Efficiency therefore matters enormously. An algorithm that feels acceptable on a paragraph of text can become unusable when applied to billions of documents or terabytes of genomic data. String algorithms demonstrate particularly well how theoretical improvements translate directly into practical impact.

The Naive Pattern Matching Algorithm

The naive string-matching algorithm is the most straightforward approach imaginable. Given a text and a pattern, the algorithm aligns the pattern with the beginning of the text and compares characters one by one. If all characters match, a match is reported. If a mismatch occurs, the pattern is shifted one position to the right and the process repeats.

This algorithm is easy to understand, easy to implement, and easy to reason about. Its simplicity makes it an excellent starting point for building intuition. Unfortunately, that same simplicity hides serious inefficiency.

In the worst case, the naive algorithm compares nearly every character of the pattern against nearly every character of the text. When texts are long and patterns are repetitive, the number of comparisons grows rapidly, revealing the algorithm's limitations.

Visualizing Naive Matching

Visualization makes the inefficiency of naive matching immediately clear. Each shift of the pattern restarts comparisons from the beginning, even when previous comparisons already revealed useful information. The algorithm behaves as if it has no memory, repeatedly rediscovering the same mismatches.

This lack of reuse is exactly what more advanced string algorithms aim to fix.

Learning from Failure: Where Naive Matching Breaks Down

Consider searching for a pattern like "ABABAC" within a long text containing repeated "ABABA" sequences. The naive algorithm repeatedly matches most of the pattern before failing at the last character, only to start over one position later. This scenario highlights the core inefficiency: the algorithm ignores partial progress.

Understanding this failure case prepares you to appreciate why smarter algorithms behave differently.

The Key Insight: Patterns Contain Structure

More advanced string-matching algorithms succeed because they treat the pattern itself as data worth analyzing. Instead of blindly comparing characters, they ask what the pattern reveals about itself. Repeated prefixes, suffixes, and character distributions can all be exploited to skip unnecessary work.

This shift in perspective, from text-centered to pattern-aware, marks the transition from naive methods to algorithmic cleverness.

Knuth-Morris-Pratt (KMP): Remembering Progress

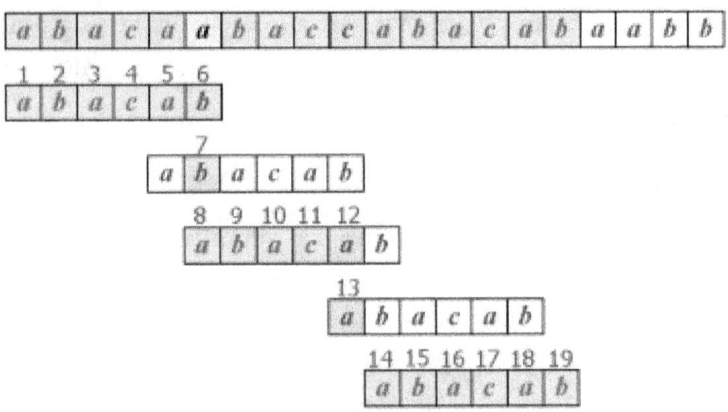

x	0	1	2	3	4	5
P[x]	*a*	*b*	*a*	*c*	*a*	*b*
f(x)	0	0	1	0	1	2

The Knuth-Morris-Pratt algorithm, commonly abbreviated as KMP, addresses naive matching's biggest weakness by avoiding redundant comparisons. When a mismatch occurs, KMP uses information about the pattern to determine how far it can shift without missing a possible match.

The core idea behind KMP is the **prefix function**, which captures how prefixes of the pattern overlap with its suffixes. This information allows the algorithm to reuse previous matches rather than discarding them.

KMP's behavior is best understood visually. Instead of resetting the pattern completely after a mismatch, the algorithm slides it to a position that preserves as much matching progress as possible.

KMP Through Visualization

Prefix tables and state diagrams make KMP far less intimidating. They show how the algorithm transitions smoothly between partial matches, never moving backward in the text. This property guarantees linear-time performance, regardless of input.

Although KMP introduces additional preprocessing, that cost is quickly repaid when searching large texts. The algorithm demonstrates how a small amount of upfront analysis can eliminate massive downstream effort.

Boyer-Moore: Looking from the Right Direction

While KMP improves matching by reusing left-to-right progress, the Boyer-Moore algorithm takes a different and often more dramatic approach. Instead of comparing the pattern from left to right, it compares characters starting from the end of the pattern.

When a mismatch occurs, Boyer-Moore uses heuristics such as the **bad character rule** and the **good suffix rule** to skip large portions of the text. In many practical cases, the algorithm jumps forward by more than the length of the pattern itself.

This behavior gives Boyer–Moore an almost counterintuitive feel, yet its effectiveness in real-world text search is well established.

Pattern Shift Diagrams and Intuition

Pattern shift diagrams are essential for understanding Boyer-Moore. They illustrate how mismatches near the end of the pattern can justify large jumps, based on where mismatched characters appear elsewhere in the pattern.

These visuals reinforce a critical lesson: sometimes the fastest way forward is not gradual progress, but informed leaps.

Automata and Theoretical Foundations

Behind algorithms like KMP lies a deeper theoretical foundation rooted in finite automata. From this perspective, pattern matching becomes a problem of state transitions driven by incoming characters.

While full automata construction can feel abstract, even a light exposure clarifies why these algorithms work. Each state represents how much of the pattern has been matched so far, and transitions encode how to proceed efficiently after each character.

This theory-practice balance is important. You do not need to become an automata expert to use string algorithms effectively, but understanding the conceptual model strengthens intuition and confidence.

Comparing String Matching Algorithms

Comparison tables make trade-offs explicit. Naive matching is simple but slow. KMP guarantees linear time but requires preprocessing. Boyer-Moore is often fastest in practice but more complex to implement. Each algorithm occupies a distinct position in the design space.

These comparisons reinforce the idea that algorithm choice depends on context, not reputation alone.

Search Engines at Scale

Modern search engines such as **Google** rely heavily on string and pattern matching, although rarely in isolation. Query processing, indexing, document scanning, and ranking all involve sophisticated text analysis built on these foundational ideas.

At scale, even small inefficiencies multiply dramatically. Efficient string algorithms therefore play a critical role in delivering results quickly and economically across billions of queries.

This case study demonstrates how textbook algorithms evolve into industrial-strength systems through careful engineering.

Applications Beyond Search

String matching algorithms power spell checkers by identifying likely corrections, bioinformatics tools by aligning DNA sequences, and plagiarism detectors by finding suspicious overlaps between documents. In each case, the core challenge is the same: identifying meaningful patterns within vast textual data.

The universality of this challenge explains why string algorithms remain an active area of research and optimization.

String Algorithm Comparison Guide

A concise comparison guide summarizing algorithm assumptions, performance characteristics, preprocessing costs, and typical use cases provides a practical reference. Such a guide helps practitioners choose wisely rather than defaulting to the most familiar method.

Reflection: Patterns as Information

String and pattern matching algorithms teach a profound lesson. Patterns are not just things to be searched for; they are sources of information that can guide the search itself. By recognizing structure within patterns, algorithms achieve efficiency that brute force cannot match.

15. Mathematical and Number-Theoretic Algorithms

Mathematics often feels abstract, distant, and theoretical, especially when first encountered through symbols and proofs. Algorithms grounded in number theory challenge that perception directly. They reveal that deep mathematical ideas do not live only on chalkboards, but power some of the most critical systems in modern computing, from secure communication to digital identity and financial transactions. This chapter connects mathematical elegance with practical necessity, showing how ideas developed centuries ago quietly shape today's technological infrastructure.

Rather than treating mathematics as a prerequisite hurdle, this chapter treats it as a toolkit. Each concept is introduced through motivation, reinforced through examples, and anchored in applications that demonstrate why the theory matters. The goal is not to turn you into a mathematician, but to help you think mathematically when designing or understanding algorithms.

Why Number Theory Appears in Algorithms

Many computational problems involve discrete objects: integers, remainders, divisibility, and primes. These objects behave differently from real numbers, and their behavior often produces surprising structure. Number theory studies these structures, and algorithms that draw on number theory exploit predictable patterns hidden within integers.

In practice, number-theoretic algorithms appear whenever problems involve security, randomness, hashing, error detection, and identity verification. These are not niche concerns. They are foundational to the trust we place in digital systems every day.

The Euclidean Algorithm: Elegance Through Simplicity

One of the most beautiful examples of a mathematical algorithm is the Euclidean algorithm for computing the greatest common divisor of two integers. Attributed to **Euclid**, this algorithm is more than two thousand years old, yet it remains central to modern computing.

The algorithm rests on a simple observation. The greatest common divisor of two numbers does not change if the larger number is replaced by its remainder when divided by the smaller. Repeating this step reduces the problem steadily until the remainder becomes zero, at which point the divisor is revealed.

What makes this algorithm remarkable is not just its correctness, but its efficiency. Each step dramatically reduces the size of the numbers involved, which explains why the algorithm runs quickly even for very large integers.

This is an early and powerful example of how mathematical insight leads directly to algorithmic efficiency.

Proof and Insight Working Together

The correctness of the Euclidean algorithm can be demonstrated through a clear mathematical argument, but its power becomes evident when you trace concrete examples. Watching large numbers collapse rapidly into smaller ones builds intuition that no formal proof alone can provide.

This balance between proof and example illustrates a broader theme of this chapter. Mathematical reasoning provides guarantees, while worked examples provide understanding. Both are essential for confident algorithm design.

Modular Arithmetic: Arithmetic with Cycles

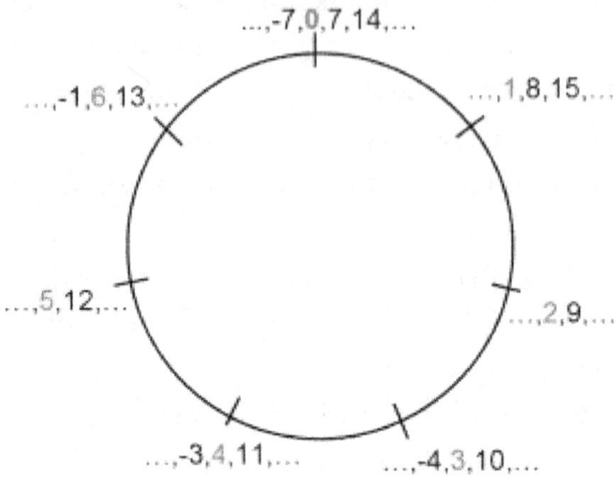

Modular arithmetic studies numbers under a wrapping behavior, where values repeat after reaching a certain modulus. Clock arithmetic is a familiar example, where hours cycle after twelve. In computing, modular arithmetic appears everywhere, from hash functions to encryption.

Algorithms based on modular arithmetic rely on predictable repetition combined with surprising complexity. Simple operations such as addition and multiplication behave differently when results are taken modulo a number, and these differences can be exploited to design efficient and secure systems.

Understanding modular arithmetic conceptually is far more important than memorizing formulas. Once you grasp the idea of arithmetic on a cycle, many cryptographic and hashing algorithms become far more approachable.

Prime Numbers and Their Special Role

Prime numbers sit at the heart of number theory. They are the building blocks of integers, yet their distribution appears irregular and unpredictable. This combination of simplicity and mystery makes primes uniquely valuable for algorithms.

From an algorithmic perspective, primes are difficult to factor but easy to multiply. This asymmetry underpins many cryptographic systems. Algorithms that generate primes, test primality, or operate on large prime numbers are therefore central to secure computing.

The difficulty of factoring large numbers is not a flaw; it is a feature that modern security depends on.

From Number Theory to Cryptography

Cryptography transforms mathematical properties into practical guarantees. It allows two parties to communicate securely over an open channel, verify identities, and protect data from unauthorized access. Number-theoretic algorithms provide the foundation for these guarantees.

Public-key cryptography is especially striking because it relies on mathematical problems that are easy in one direction and hard in the reverse direction. This one-way difficulty creates security without secrecy of the algorithm itself.

The RSA Case Study: Mathematics at Work

The RSA cryptosystem is one of the most influential applications of number theory in computing. It relies on properties of prime numbers and modular arithmetic to enable secure communication.

In RSA, large prime numbers are multiplied to form a composite number that is easy to compute but extremely difficult to factor. Encryption and decryption rely on carefully chosen exponents that interact predictably under modular arithmetic. The security of the system depends on the practical difficulty of reversing these operations without secret information.

What makes RSA especially compelling is that its core ideas can be understood with relatively elementary mathematics, yet its implications are profound. Every secure web connection, digital signature, and encrypted message carries echoes of these number-theoretic principles.

Visualizing Encryption and Decryption

Encryption flowcharts help demystify RSA. They show how plaintext is transformed into ciphertext using public information, and how the original message can only be recovered using a private key. These diagrams reinforce the idea that security emerges from structure, not obscurity.

Seeing the flow of data through mathematical transformations makes the abstract concrete and highlights the algorithmic nature of cryptography.

Mathematical Guarantees and Real-World Limits

While number theory provides strong theoretical guarantees, practical systems must still consider performance, key sizes, and implementation details. Algorithms that are secure in theory can fail if implemented carelessly or if assumptions change due to advances in hardware or mathematics.

This tension between theory and practice underscores the importance of understanding both. Mathematical rigor tells us what should work, while engineering judgment tells us how to make it work reliably in the real world.

Math Foundations Review

At this stage, it is useful to pause and review the mathematical ideas that support number-theoretic algorithms. Divisibility, remainders, prime factorization, and modular arithmetic form the core foundation. Understanding these concepts conceptually, rather than mechanically, prepares you to reason about algorithms that rely on them.

This review is not about mastering proofs, but about recognizing patterns and relationships that algorithms exploit.

Beyond Cryptography

Number-theoretic algorithms appear in error-correcting codes, random number generation, hashing, and distributed systems. In each case, mathematical structure provides reliability, predictability, or security where naïve approaches would fail.

These applications reinforce a central lesson. Pure mathematics and practical computing are not opposites. They are partners.

Reflection: Mathematics as a Design Tool

This final chapter completes a journey that began with simple step-by-step procedures and ends with mathematically grounded systems that protect global communication. Mathematical algorithms remind us that elegance and utility are not competing goals. When theory and application are balanced thoughtfully, algorithms achieve both beauty and impact.

With this foundation, you now have a complete algorithmic toolkit, spanning intuitive problem solving, structured design, efficiency analysis, and mathematical rigor. The next step is not merely to apply these algorithms, but to recognize where new ones are needed, and to design them with the same balance of clarity, efficiency, and insight that you have seen throughout this book.

16. Randomized and Probabilistic Algorithms

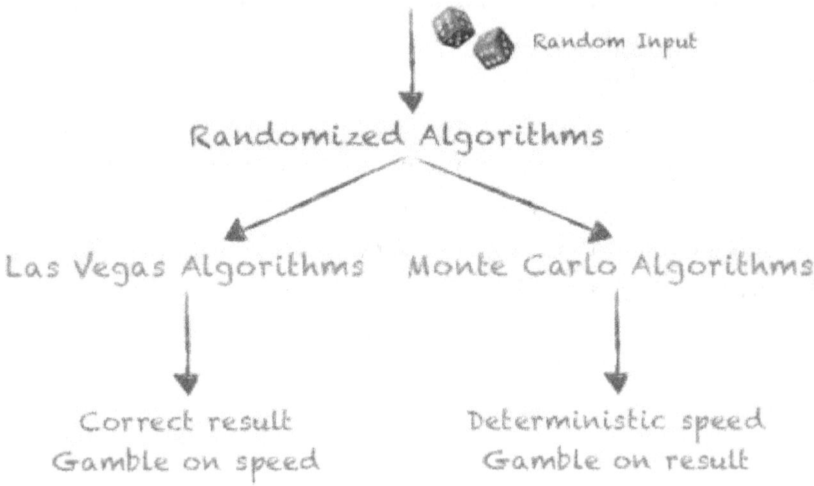

At first glance, randomness appears to be the opposite of what algorithms represent. Algorithms are supposed to be precise, repeatable, and predictable, while randomness feels noisy and unreliable. This apparent contradiction is exactly what makes randomized and probabilistic algorithms so powerful. By deliberately introducing randomness as a **computational resource**, algorithms can avoid worst-case scenarios, simplify design, and achieve performance guarantees that deterministic approaches struggle to match.

This chapter develops probabilistic thinking gradually and intuitively. Rather than assuming a strong background in probability, we begin by building intuition about randomness and expectation. From there, we explore how randomization improves classical algorithms, compare Monte Carlo and Las Vegas approaches, and examine how large-scale systems use randomness in practice. The goal is not to replace deterministic thinking, but to expand your toolkit with methods that embrace uncertainty productively.

Why Randomness Helps Algorithms

Deterministic algorithms follow a fixed path for a given input. This predictability is often desirable, but it can also be a weakness. Certain inputs can consistently trigger worst-case behavior, leading to poor performance even when average behavior is excellent.

Randomized algorithms break this predictability intentionally. By making random choices during execution, they ensure that no single input can reliably force worst-case behavior. Instead of asking for guaranteed performance in every case, randomized algorithms offer strong guarantees **on average** or **with high probability**, which is often more than sufficient in real systems.

This shift in perspective is subtle but profound. We stop demanding absolute certainty and begin managing risk intelligently.

A Gentle Probability Refresher

Before diving into algorithms, it helps to review a few probabilistic ideas that appear repeatedly. Probability measures the likelihood of an event occurring, expressed as a value between zero and one. Expected value represents a weighted average outcome, capturing what happens over many repetitions rather than in a single trial.

In algorithm design, expected value often matters more than worst-case outcomes. If an algorithm runs quickly almost all the time and only rarely performs poorly, it may be preferable to a deterministic algorithm with slower but guaranteed performance. This idea underlies much of randomized algorithm design.

Randomness as a Design Tool

Randomness is not used because we lack better ideas. It is used because it simplifies reasoning about complex systems. When random choices are made carefully, they smooth out irregularities in input data and distribute work more evenly.

Randomized algorithms are often shorter, easier to implement, and easier to analyze than their deterministic counterparts. Their correctness may be probabilistic, but their efficiency is often superior in practice.

Randomized Quicksort: A Familiar Example Revisited

Quicksort is a fast-sorting algorithm whose performance depends heavily on pivot selection. Deterministic pivot choices can lead to highly unbalanced partitions for certain inputs, degrading performance significantly.

Randomized quicksort solves this problem by choosing the pivot at random. This simple change ensures that no adversarial input can consistently force bad behavior. While the algorithm does not guarantee optimal partitions every time, its expected running time is excellent.

This example illustrates a recurring pattern. Randomization does not eliminate bad cases, but it makes them rare and uncorrelated.

Monte Carlo Algorithms: Fast but Probabilistic

Monte Carlo algorithms always run quickly, but they may produce incorrect results with a small probability. The defining feature is that their running time is fixed or bounded, while correctness is probabilistic.

An example is a randomized algorithm for testing whether a number is prime. Such algorithms can quickly identify non-prime numbers and declare a number prime with extremely high confidence, even though absolute certainty is not guaranteed.

In practice, the probability of error can be made so small that it becomes irrelevant. Monte Carlo methods are widely used when speed is critical and occasional error is tolerable.

Las Vegas Algorithms: Correctness Guaranteed

Las Vegas algorithms, by contrast, always produce correct results, but their running time is probabilistic. They may take longer on some runs and shorter on others, but they never compromise correctness.

Randomized quicksort is a classic Las Vegas algorithm. It always sorts correctly, but the exact number of comparisons depends on random choices made during execution. Expected performance is excellent, even though individual runs may vary.

This distinction between Monte Carlo and Las Vegas algorithms clarifies how randomness can be applied differently depending on requirements.

Visualizing Expected Performance

Graphs of expected value help demystify probabilistic guarantees. Instead of focusing on the slowest possible run, we look at average behavior across many runs. These visualizations show how rare worst-case events become statistically insignificant as input size grows.

This way of thinking aligns naturally with real-world systems, where algorithms run millions or billions of times and average behavior dominates experience.

Randomized Data Structures

Randomization is not limited to algorithms; it also enhances data structures. Hash tables rely on randomization, either explicitly or implicitly, to distribute keys evenly and avoid clustering. Skip lists use random levels to achieve balanced behavior similar to trees, but with simpler implementation.

These structures demonstrate how randomness can replace complex balancing logic with probabilistic guarantees that are easier to maintain.

Randomization in Recommendation Systems

Large-scale platforms rely heavily on randomness to improve user experience and system robustness. Services such as **Netflix** use randomization in recommendation pipelines to explore new content, avoid feedback loops, and measure user preferences through controlled experimentation.

By occasionally showing users content outside their predicted preferences, the system gathers better data and avoids becoming overly confident in narrow predictions. Randomness here serves as a learning mechanism rather than a source of noise.

This case study highlights how probabilistic algorithms operate at the intersection of computation, data, and human behavior.

Probability Distributions in Practice

Randomized algorithms often depend on specific probability distributions. Uniform distributions ensure fairness, while biased distributions can emphasize exploration or exploitation. Understanding how these distributions shape algorithm behavior is more important than memorizing formulas.

Visualization of distributions helps explain why some random choices lead to better balance and performance than others.

When Randomization Is Especially Valuable

Randomization shines when worst-case inputs are hard to predict, when adversarial behavior is possible, or when simplicity is a priority. It is also valuable when approximate answers are acceptable or when average-case performance matters more than guarantees for every instance.

Recognizing these scenarios helps you decide when randomness should be introduced deliberately.

Randomization Benefits Checklist

Randomized algorithms reduce sensitivity to input patterns, simplify design, improve expected performance, and often scale more gracefully. They trade absolute certainty for efficiency and robustness, a trade that is frequently worthwhile in large systems.

This checklist serves as a reminder that randomness is a strategic choice, not a last resort.

Limitations and Responsible Use

Randomized algorithms are not universally appropriate. Systems requiring strict reproducibility or absolute correctness may reject probabilistic outcomes. Debugging can also be more challenging when behavior varies between runs.

Understanding these limitations ensures that randomization is applied thoughtfully rather than blindly.

Reflection: Embracing Uncertainty Productively

Randomized and probabilistic algorithms teach an important lesson about computation. Certainty is not always necessary, and unpredictability can be a strength rather than a weakness. By embracing randomness with discipline and insight, algorithm designers can achieve performance and simplicity that deterministic thinking alone cannot provide.

With this chapter, your exploration of algorithmic design strategies is complete. You have seen how clarity, structure, efficiency, memory, exploration, mathematics, and randomness each contribute to powerful solutions. Together, they form a rich and flexible foundation for understanding and designing algorithms in a complex and ever-changing world.

17. Approximation Algorithms

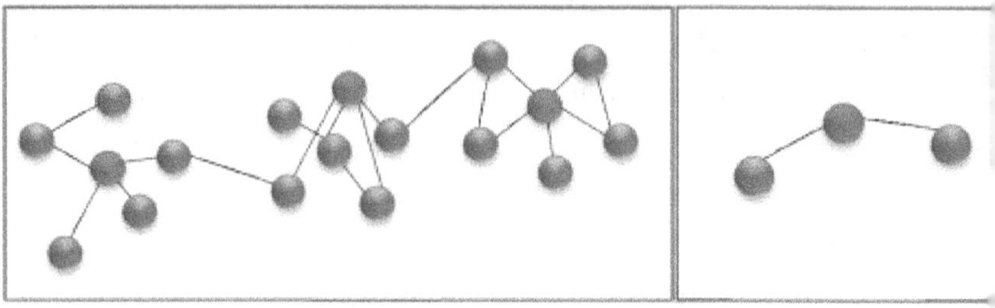

(a) (b)

As algorithm designers gain experience, they eventually encounter a sobering reality. Some problems resist exact solutions, not because we lack cleverness or computing power, but because their structure makes efficient exact computation fundamentally unlikely. Approximation algorithms emerge from this reality, not as a compromise born of weakness, but as a **pragmatic engineering response** to computational intractability.

This chapter reframes approximation as a sign of maturity in algorithm design. Instead of asking for perfection in situations where perfection is prohibitively expensive, we ask a more productive question: *how close to optimal do we need to be, and at what cost?* By understanding NP-completeness accessibly and exploring approximation techniques through real-world case studies, you will learn why "good enough" is often not only sufficient, but optimal from a systems perspective.

When Exact Solutions Become Impractical

Many of the algorithms studied earlier in this book scale beautifully. Searching, sorting, graph traversal, and dynamic programming often provide exact answers efficiently. However, some problems behave very differently. As input size grows, the number of possible solutions explodes combinatorially, overwhelming even the fastest machines.

These problems are not rare curiosities. They appear in scheduling, logistics, network design, resource allocation, and planning. Attempting to solve them exactly often leads to algorithms that work only for toy inputs and fail catastrophically at realistic scales.

Approximation algorithms exist because real systems cannot afford to wait for exact answers that may never arrive.

NP-Completeness Without Fear

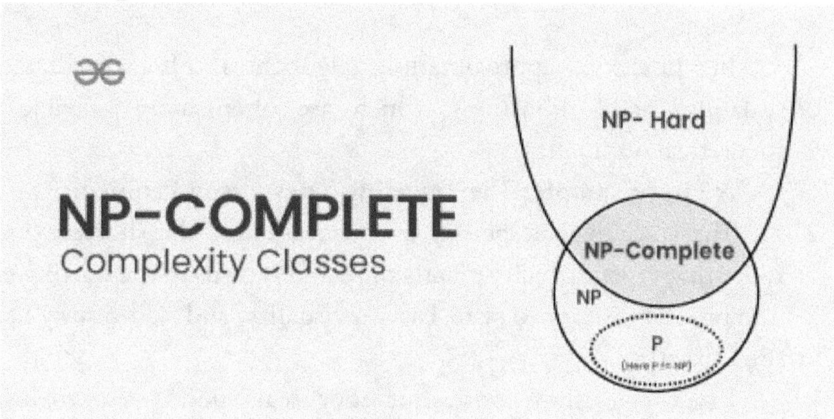

The concept of NP-completeness is often introduced with intimidating formality, but its core idea is intuitive. An NP-complete problem is one for which no efficient exact algorithm is known, and for which finding such an algorithm would imply efficient solutions for a vast class of other hard problems.

What matters most for practitioners is not the formal definition, but the implication. If a problem is NP-complete, it is widely believed that no algorithm can solve all instances optimally in polynomial time. This belief is not based on lack of effort; it is supported by decades of research and deep theoretical connections.

Recognizing NP-completeness early prevents wasted effort and encourages more productive approaches.

Approximation as an Engineering Mindset

Approximation algorithms accept that optimality may be out of reach, but they refuse to give up structure and guarantees. Instead of exact answers, they provide solutions that are provably close to optimal, often within a known factor called the **approximation ratio**.

This ratio quantifies how far the algorithm's solution can deviate from the best possible solution. Knowing this bound allows engineers to reason about tradeoffs explicitly, rather than relying on hope or intuition.

In practice, approximation algorithms offer predictability, scalability, and robustness, which are often more valuable than theoretical optimality.

A First Example: The Traveling Salesperson Problem

The traveling salesperson problem asks for the shortest possible route that visits each city exactly once and returns to the starting point. The problem is easy to state, easy to visualize, and notoriously hard to solve exactly.

Exact algorithms exist, but they scale poorly. Approximation algorithms, by contrast, can quickly produce routes that are close to optimal. While the route may not be perfect, it is often more than sufficient for practical use, especially when the alternative is no solution at all.

Visualization of approximation ratios makes this idea concrete. A slightly longer route may cost a few extra kilometers, but save hours or days of computation.

Understanding Approximation Ratios Visually

Approximation ratio diagrams show how solution quality compares to the unknown optimal solution. Instead of asking whether an answer is correct or incorrect, we ask how close it is to the best possible answer.

This shift in evaluation mindset is crucial. Approximation algorithms are judged not by perfection, but by consistency and bounded error.

Delivery Optimization: A Real-World Case Study

Large-scale delivery systems face problems that closely resemble NP-hard optimization challenges. Routing vehicles, scheduling deliveries, and balancing workloads must all happen under time pressure and uncertainty.

Companies such as **Amazon** rely on approximation and heuristic algorithms to plan delivery routes across massive networks. Exact optimization would be computationally infeasible given the number of packages, destinations, constraints, and real-time changes.

In this context, a solution that is within a few percent of optimal, but computed quickly and reliably, is vastly superior to an exact solution that arrives too late to be useful.

Why "Good Enough" Often Is Good Enough

In engineering systems, the cost of computation is part of the problem. Spending excessive time optimizing a route that saves a marginal amount of distance may cost more in computation, delay, or complexity than it saves in fuel.

Approximation algorithms align naturally with these realities. They trade small losses in optimality for large gains in speed, scalability, and simplicity. This tradeoff is not a failure; it is an informed design choice.

Common NP-Hard Problems and Their Approximations

Problems such as vertex cover, set cover, and scheduling all admit approximation algorithms with known performance bounds. These algorithms do not solve the hardest cases optimally, but they provide reliable solutions across all inputs.

Seeing multiple examples reinforces a pattern. When problems involve combinatorial explosion, approximation often emerges as the most responsible solution strategy.

Hardness Recognition Guide

Recognizing when a problem is likely to be NP-hard is a critical skill. Warning signs include exponential growth in possibilities, constraints that interact globally rather than locally, and strong similarity to known hard problems.

This recognition guide helps shift focus early from exact algorithms to approximation, heuristics, or problem reformulation, saving time and effort.

Approximation vs Heuristics

Approximation algorithms differ from heuristics in an important way. Heuristics may work well in practice, but offer no guarantees. Approximation algorithms provide mathematical bounds on solution quality.

In many systems, a hybrid approach is used. Approximation algorithms provide a baseline guarantee, while heuristics refine solutions further when time permits. Understanding this distinction helps you design systems that are both effective and trustworthy.

Philosophy: Choosing Practical Solutions

Approximation algorithms embody a broader philosophy of algorithm design. They accept limits without surrendering rigor. They value usefulness over perfection and recognize that real-world systems operate under constraints that theory alone cannot ignore.

This philosophy is not about settling for less. It is about choosing solutions that actually work.

Reflection: Wisdom in Imperfection

Approximation algorithms teach an important final lesson. Intelligence in algorithm design is not measured by how close you get to perfection, but by how well you balance correctness, efficiency, and reality. By embracing practical solutions when exact ones are out of reach, you demonstrate not weakness, but engineering wisdom.

With this chapter, the book completes its exploration of algorithmic strategies, from exact and elegant methods to probabilistic and approximate approaches. Together, they form a complete and realistic view of what algorithms can achieve, and how thoughtful designers choose among them.

18. Parallel and Distributed Algorithms

As data volumes grow and user expectations rise, algorithm designers confront a fundamental physical limit. Individual processors no longer become dramatically faster each year, yet the problems we want to solve continue to grow in size and urgency. Parallel and distributed algorithms arise from this tension. They do not attempt to solve bigger problems by running faster on a single machine. Instead, they solve them by **working together**, coordinating many processors, machines, or entire data centers toward a shared goal.

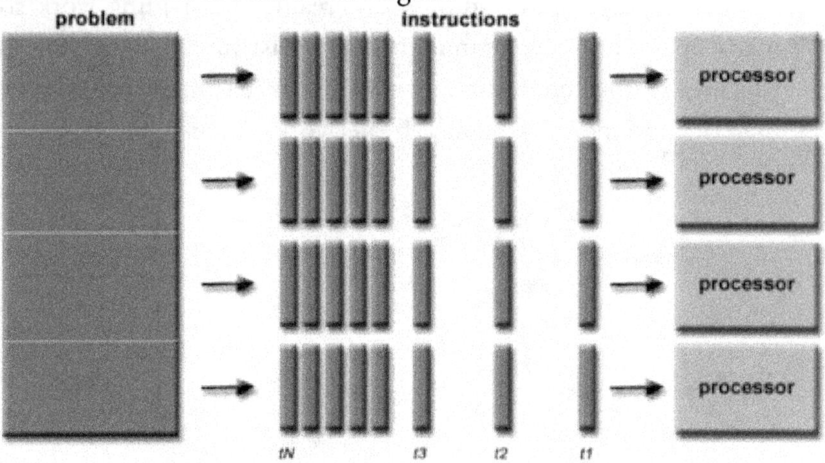

This chapter presents parallelism as a scaling solution rather than a niche optimization. We begin by building intuition about why sequential algorithms reach their limits. From there, we introduce parallel thinking, explore the MapReduce framework as an accessible model, and examine how large-scale systems transform algorithmic ideas into global infrastructure. Throughout the chapter, theoretical models are balanced carefully with the realities of modern cloud computing.

Why Sequential Algorithms Stop Scaling

Traditional algorithms are often designed with a single processor in mind. They assume one stream of execution, one memory hierarchy, and one clock driving progress forward. For many years, faster processors compensated for inefficient designs, masking scalability problems.

That era has ended. Power constraints, heat dissipation, and physical limits have slowed single-core performance improvements. As a result, simply waiting for faster hardware is no longer a viable strategy. To continue scaling, computation must be spread across multiple processing units.

Parallel algorithms address this reality by dividing work so that many operations occur simultaneously. Distributed algorithms extend this idea further, coordinating work across machines that do not share memory and may be separated by networks, latency, and failure.

Thinking in Parallel

Parallel thinking requires a shift in perspective. Instead of asking how to perform a task as efficiently as possible step by step, you ask how the task can be decomposed so that many steps can happen at the same time. This decomposition is not always obvious, and not all problems benefit equally from parallelism.

Some tasks are embarrassingly parallel, meaning they can be divided with almost no coordination. Others contain inherent dependencies that limit how much parallel speedup is possible. Understanding these boundaries is essential for effective parallel algorithm design.

Sequential vs Parallel: A Simple Comparison

Consider summing a large array of numbers. A sequential algorithm processes elements one by one. A parallel algorithm divides the array into chunks, sums each chunk independently, and then combines the partial sums.

This example highlights the basic structure of many parallel algorithms: **divide the data, compute locally, then combine globally**. The challenge lies not in the idea itself, but in managing coordination, communication, and synchronization efficiently.

Visual comparisons between sequential and parallel execution timelines make these differences immediately apparent and reinforce the intuition behind speedup.

The Cost of Coordination

Parallelism is not free. Communication between processors takes time. Synchronization introduces waiting. Load imbalance leaves some processors idle while others work.

These costs explain why parallel algorithms often show diminishing returns as more processors are added. Beyond a certain point, overhead dominates useful work. This reality is captured by theoretical results such as Amdahl's Law, which reminds us that even small sequential portions of an algorithm can limit overall speedup.

Effective parallel algorithms minimize coordination while maximizing independent work.

Shared Memory and Distributed Memory Models

Parallel algorithms are often classified by how processors communicate. In shared-memory models, all processors access the same memory space, which simplifies communication but introduces challenges related to consistency and contention.

In distributed-memory models, each processor has its own memory, and communication occurs explicitly through messages. This model reflects the structure of clusters and cloud systems, where machines are connected by networks rather than shared memory.

Understanding these models clarifies why algorithms designed for one environment may not translate directly to the other.

MapReduce: A Practical Entry Point

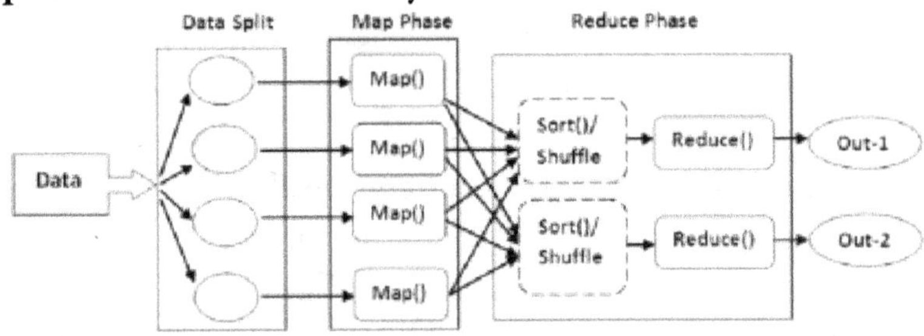

MapReduce provides an accessible framework for understanding distributed algorithms. It abstracts away many low-level details and allows programmers to focus on two core operations: mapping and reducing.

In the map phase, data is processed independently in parallel, transforming input records into intermediate key value pairs. In the reduce phase, all values associated with the same key are combined to produce final results.

This simple abstraction supports a wide range of tasks, including counting, aggregation, indexing, and data transformation. Its power lies in enforcing a structure that naturally scales across thousands of machines.

Why MapReduce Works So Well

MapReduce succeeds because it aligns with the strengths of distributed systems. It minimizes communication, tolerates failures, and encourages stateless computation. By restricting how data flows through the system, it enables aggressive optimization behind the scenes.

From an algorithmic perspective, MapReduce illustrates how limiting expressive power can actually increase scalability. By giving up arbitrary communication patterns, algorithms gain reliability and performance at massive scale.

Google's Infrastructure: Algorithms at Planetary Scale

Few organizations demonstrate the impact of parallel and distributed algorithms more clearly than **Google**. Search indexing, web crawling, data analytics, and machine learning workloads all rely on distributed computation across global data centers.

Google's infrastructure shows how abstract ideas become concrete systems. Fault tolerance, replication, load balancing, and distributed scheduling are not optional features; they are essential components of algorithms that operate continuously at planetary scale.

This case study serves not as an implementation guide, but as inspiration. It demonstrates what becomes possible when algorithmic thinking embraces distribution fully.

Parallel Sorting and Searching

Sorting and searching provide familiar examples that translate naturally into parallel contexts. Large datasets can be partitioned, sorted locally, and then merged. Searches can be distributed across shards, dramatically reducing response time.

These algorithms illustrate an important pattern. Parallelism often works best when combined with data partitioning strategies that reduce the need for global coordination.

Distributed Failures as a Design Constraint

In distributed systems, failure is not an exception; it is expected. Machines crash, networks partition, and messages are delayed or lost. Distributed algorithms must therefore be designed with resilience in mind.

This requirement changes how correctness is defined. Instead of assuming perfect execution, algorithms must guarantee progress and consistency even when components fail. This reality introduces tradeoffs between availability, consistency, and performance that shape modern systems.

Parallelization Checklist

Before parallelizing an algorithm, it is essential to ask structured questions. Can the work be decomposed into largely independent tasks? Are data dependencies minimal or manageable? Is communication cost small relative to computation? Can failures be detected and handled gracefully?

This checklist helps distinguish problems that benefit from parallelism from those that do not, preventing unnecessary complexity.

Cloud Computing as the New Default

Parallel and distributed algorithms now operate primarily in cloud environments. Elastic resources, on-demand scaling, and managed infrastructure have changed how algorithms are deployed and evaluated.

Designing algorithms for the cloud means embracing heterogeneity, latency, and dynamic resource allocation. Algorithms must adapt not just to data, but to changing execution environments.

Balancing Theory and Practice

Theoretical models provide insight into limits and possibilities, while practical systems reveal hidden costs and constraints. Effective designers move fluidly between these perspectives, using theory to guide design and practice to refine it.

Parallel and distributed algorithms exemplify this balance more than any other topic in computer science.

Reflection: Thinking at System Scale

Parallel and distributed algorithms expand algorithmic thinking beyond individual procedures into system-wide coordination. They teach you to reason about performance, reliability, and scalability simultaneously.

As computing continues to move toward larger, more interconnected systems, this way of thinking becomes indispensable. Algorithms are no longer just instructions for machines. They are blueprints for cooperation at scale.

19. Machine Learning Algorithms

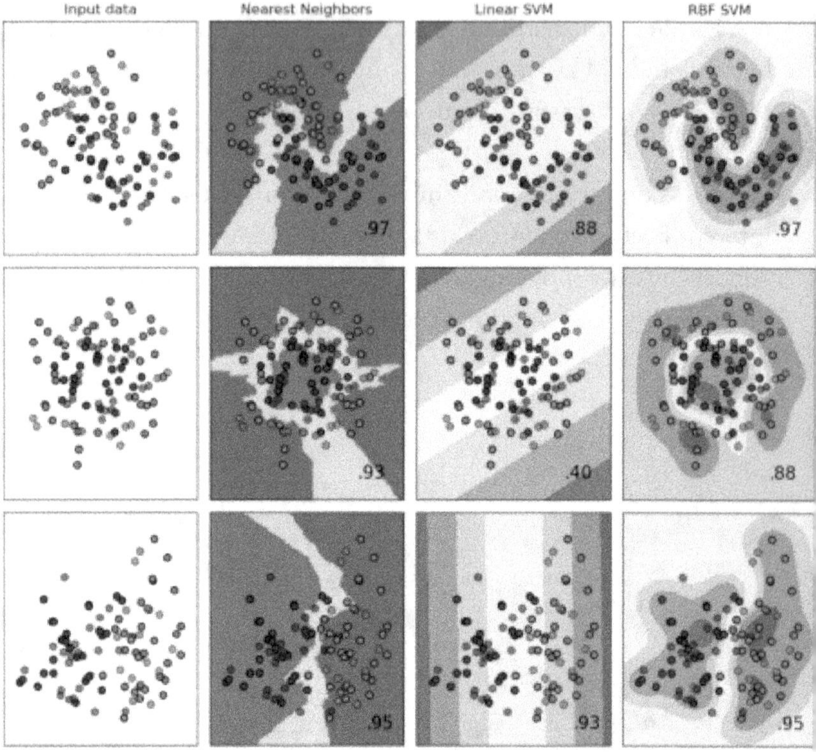

Machine learning algorithms represent a shift in how problems are solved computationally. Instead of writing explicit step-by-step rules that describe exactly how a solution should be produced, we design algorithms that **learn patterns from data** and improve their behavior through experience. This shift does not abandon algorithmic thinking; rather, it extends it. At their core, machine learning methods are still algorithms, governed by logic, optimization, and computational constraints.

This chapter introduces machine learning from an algorithmic perspective. The focus is not on mastering complex models or advanced mathematics, but on understanding how learning algorithms behave, why they work, and when they are appropriate. By grounding ideas in small, interpretable datasets and visual explanations, we build intuition first and formality second. A real-world case study from music recommendation demonstrates how these ideas operate at scale.

From Rule-Based to Data-Driven Algorithms

Traditional algorithms rely on explicit instructions crafted by humans. If the rules are correct and complete, the algorithm behaves correctly. However, many real-world problems resist this approach. Human language, user preferences, images, and sound are difficult to describe precisely using fixed rules.

Machine learning algorithms address this difficulty by shifting responsibility from the programmer to the data. Instead of encoding every rule, we provide examples, and the algorithm infers patterns that generalize beyond those examples. This approach is powerful, but it introduces new challenges related to data quality, uncertainty, and interpretability.

From an algorithmic standpoint, learning becomes an optimization process. The algorithm searches for parameters or structures that best explain observed data according to a defined objective.

What Makes an Algorithm "Learning-Based"

A machine learning algorithm typically consists of three components. There is a representation, which defines the space of possible models. There is an objective function, which measures how well a model fits the data. There is an optimization procedure, which searches for a model that minimizes error or maximizes performance.

These components mirror ideas you have already encountered. Optimization appears in dynamic programming and approximation algorithms. Search appears in graph traversal and backtracking. What changes in machine learning is that the objective is defined statistically, and success is measured probabilistically rather than deterministically.

Supervised Learning: Learning from Examples

Supervised learning algorithms learn from labeled data, where each example includes both input and desired output. The goal is to learn a mapping that predicts outputs accurately for new, unseen inputs.

Linear Regression as a First Learning Algorithm

Linear regression is one of the simplest learning algorithms, yet it captures many essential ideas. Given pairs of inputs and outputs, the algorithm finds a line that best fits the data according to a defined error metric.

Visualizing this process reveals its algorithmic nature. The algorithm adjusts parameters gradually, reducing error step by step. Even in this simple setting, we see the tradeoff between underfitting, where the model is too simple, and overfitting, where the model captures noise rather than structure.

Linear regression demonstrates that learning is not magic. It is systematic search guided by data.

Classification and Decision Boundaries

Classification algorithms assign inputs to discrete categories. Examples include spam detection, image labeling, and sentiment analysis. From an algorithmic perspective, classification involves learning **decision boundaries** that separate regions of input space.

Simple classifiers such as nearest-neighbor methods rely on distance computations and local comparisons, which connect directly to searching algorithms. More structured classifiers introduce boundaries that are learned through optimization.

Decision boundary visualizations make these ideas concrete. They show how algorithms partition space based on observed patterns and why some boundaries generalize better than others.

Unsupervised Learning: Discovering Structure

Unsupervised learning algorithms operate without labeled outputs. Instead of predicting known answers, they seek to uncover hidden structure within data.

Clustering as Algorithmic Grouping

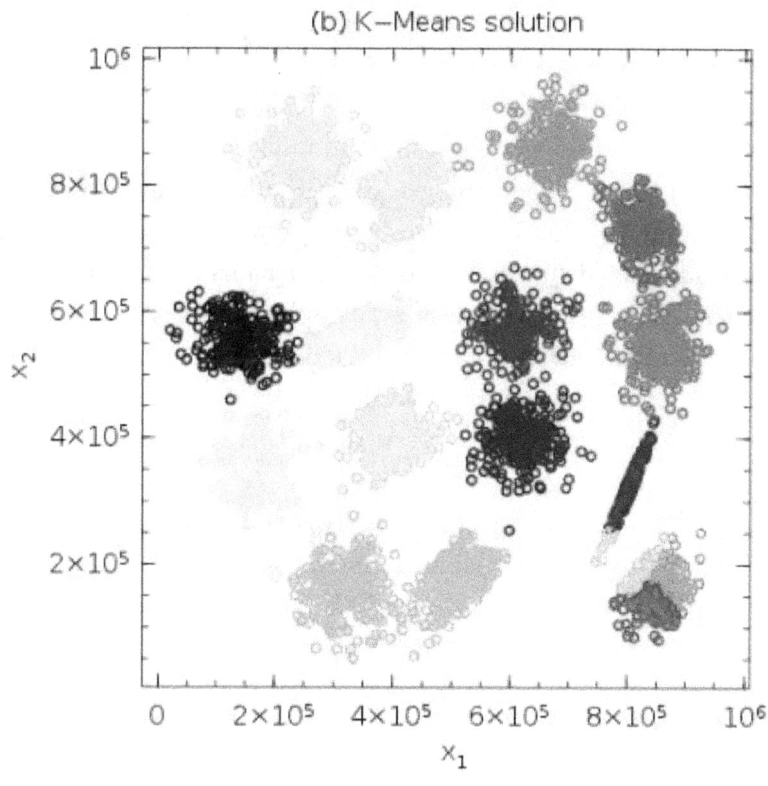

Clustering algorithms group data points based on similarity. From an algorithmic perspective, clustering is a form of partitioning that balances internal cohesion with external separation.

Simple clustering methods such as k-means rely on iterative refinement. The algorithm alternates between assigning points to clusters and updating cluster centers. This process resembles optimization algorithms you have already studied, where repeated local improvements lead to a stable solution.

Clustering visualizations help explain both the power and the fragility of these algorithms. Small changes in data or initialization can lead to different outcomes, highlighting the probabilistic nature of learning.

Learning as Optimization

Across machine learning methods, optimization plays a central role. Algorithms repeatedly evaluate a model, measure error, and adjust parameters. This process echoes ideas from gradient descent, approximation algorithms, and randomized methods.

Understanding learning as optimization clarifies why training can be slow, why local optima matter, and why randomness is often introduced deliberately. These behaviors are not flaws, but consequences of searching large, complex spaces.

Generalization: The Central Challenge

A learning algorithm's true goal is not to perform well on training data, but to generalize to new data. This requirement distinguishes machine learning from memorization.

Algorithmically, generalization depends on controlling complexity. Models that are too flexible can memorize noise, while models that are too rigid fail to capture structure. Balancing this tradeoff is one of the defining challenges of machine learning design.

This balance echo's themes from earlier chapters, where efficiency and approximation required careful tradeoffs rather than absolute guarantees.

Recommendation Systems: A Case Study

Music recommendation systems provide a compelling example of machine learning in action. Platforms such as **Spotify** use learning algorithms to suggest songs, playlists, and artists tailored to individual users.

From an algorithmic perspective, recommendations involve pattern recognition across massive datasets. Listening histories, user interactions, and item similarities form a large, evolving dataset.

Learning algorithms identify correlations and preferences, updating models continuously as new data arrives.

This case study demonstrates that machine learning algorithms are not isolated components. They operate within larger systems that handle data collection, evaluation, and feedback, blending learning with traditional algorithmic infrastructure.

Why Machine Learning Algorithms Scale

Machine learning algorithms often scale well because they are designed to work with approximate solutions and statistical guarantees. Exact answers are neither required nor expected. Instead, performance is evaluated empirically across many instances.

This mindset aligns naturally with distributed and parallel computing. Training can be divided across machines, and predictions can be made independently, enabling large-scale deployment.

ML Algorithm Selector

Choosing a machine learning algorithm depends on data characteristics, problem type, interpretability requirements, and computational constraints. Simple models may outperform complex ones on small or noisy datasets. Unsupervised methods are appropriate when labels are unavailable. Supervised methods dominate when reliable examples exist.

This selector encourages thoughtful choice rather than defaulting to fashionable techniques.

Limits and Responsibilities

Machine learning algorithms inherit biases from data, amplify patterns that may be undesirable, and sometimes behave unpredictably. From an algorithmic standpoint, these issues arise because learning systems optimize objectives that may not capture broader human values.

Recognizing these limitations is part of responsible algorithm design. Machine learning does not replace judgment; it demands it.

Reflection: Algorithms That Adapt

Machine learning algorithms represent a natural extension of algorithmic thinking into uncertain, data-rich environments. They replace rigid instruction with adaptive behavior, while remaining grounded in optimization, structure, and computation.

By viewing machine learning as a family of algorithms rather than a mysterious black box, you gain the ability to reason about its strengths, limitations, and appropriate use. This perspective completes the book's exploration of algorithms, bringing together structure, efficiency, probability, approximation, and learning into a unified view of modern computation.

20. Computational Geometry

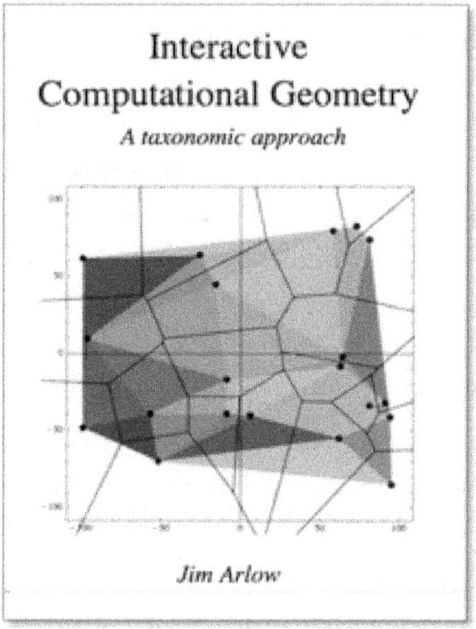

Computational geometry studies algorithms that reason about **space, shape, and position**. While many algorithms operate on numbers or symbols, geometric algorithms operate on points, lines, polygons, and surfaces. These algorithms answer questions such as where objects are located, how they intersect, how space can be partitioned, and how movement can be planned safely and efficiently.

This chapter develops spatial intuition first and formalism second. By grounding ideas in two-dimensional geometry, we build accessibility and visual clarity. From there, we extend concepts into three dimensions, where the same principles power sophisticated applications such as robotics, graphics, and geographic information systems. A case study from autonomous vehicles demonstrates how geometric algorithms move directly from theory into life-critical real-world systems.

Why Geometry Is Algorithmic

Geometry is often taught as static diagrams and formulas. Computational geometry transforms it into a dynamic process. Instead of asking what *is* true about a shape, we ask how a computer can *decide* what is true, efficiently and robustly.

Geometric algorithms are essential whenever software must interact with the physical world or visually represent information. Screens, maps, cameras, sensors, and robots all produce spatial data. Turning that data into decisions requires algorithms that can reason precisely about geometry under uncertainty and scale.

Points, Lines, and Space as Data

At the core of computational geometry lie simple primitives. Points represent locations. Line segments represent connections or paths. Polygons represent boundaries and regions. Although these objects are mathematically simple, algorithmic challenges arise because of precision, edge cases, and combinatorial complexity.

Even basic questions such as whether two-line segments intersect require careful algorithmic treatment. Floating-point errors, degenerate cases, and performance constraints make naïve approaches unreliable in practice.

Geometry Primitives Reference

Before exploring full algorithms, it is useful to establish a shared vocabulary of geometric primitives. Points define position. Vectors encode direction and displacement. Line segments connect points. Angles describe orientation. Polygons define enclosed regions. Distances and orientations provide the quantitative relationships between these objects.

Nearly every geometric algorithm is built by combining these primitives carefully and consistently.

Line Segment Intersection: A Foundational Problem

Determining whether two-line segments intersect is one of the most fundamental problems in computational geometry. It appears in graphics rendering, collision detection, map overlays, and robotics.

The challenge lies not in drawing the segments, but in computing intersection reliably under all conditions. Algorithms must handle parallel lines, shared endpoints, overlapping segments, and numerical imprecision. Visual step-by-step diagrams make it clear how orientation tests and cross products are used to resolve these cases.

This problem illustrates a recurring theme: simple geometric questions often hide subtle algorithmic complexity.

Convex Hulls: Wrapping Space Efficiently

The convex hull of a set of points is the smallest convex polygon that contains all of them. Intuitively, it is what you get if you stretch a rubber band around the outside of the points.

Convex hull algorithms are central to many applications, including shape analysis, collision detection, and pattern recognition. By reducing a complex point set to its outer boundary, these algorithms simplify subsequent computation dramatically.

Two-dimensional convex hull algorithms are especially instructive because they combine geometric intuition with algorithmic efficiency. Visual hull-construction diagrams make it easy to see how interior points are discarded while boundary points remain.

Spatial Partitioning and Proximity

Many geometric problems involve proximity. Which point is closest. Which region contains a query point. Which objects might collide.

Spatial partitioning algorithms address these questions by dividing space into manageable regions. Structures such as grids, trees, and diagrams allow algorithms to ignore large portions of space that are irrelevant to a given query.

Voronoi diagrams provide a particularly elegant example. They partition space based on proximity to a set of points, producing regions that capture nearest-neighbor relationships visually and algorithmically.

From Two Dimensions to Three

Most geometric intuition begins in two dimensions, where diagrams are easy to draw and reason about. However, real-world systems often operate in three dimensions. Extending algorithms from 2D to 3D introduces new challenges, including increased computational complexity and more intricate edge cases.

Despite these challenges, the same core ideas persist. Points become vectors in space. Polygons become polyhedral. Distances and orientations still guide decisions. Understanding 2D geometry thoroughly provides a strong foundation for reasoning in higher dimensions.

Autonomous Vehicles: Geometry in Motion

Autonomous vehicles rely heavily on computational geometry to perceive and navigate their environment. Sensors produce clouds of points representing obstacles, lanes, pedestrians, and other vehicles. Algorithms must interpret this spatial data in real time to make safe decisions.

Companies such as **Tesla** integrate geometric algorithms into perception, mapping, and motion planning systems. Lane detection uses line and curve fitting.

Obstacle avoidance relies on collision detection and distance computation. Route planning involves geometric reasoning over maps and trajectories.

This case study highlights why geometric correctness is not optional. Errors are not merely inefficient; they are dangerous.

Motion Planning and Collision Avoidance

One of the most demanding applications of computational geometry is motion planning. The goal is to find a path from a start position to a goal position without intersecting obstacles.

Algorithmically, this involves reasoning about free space, boundaries, and constraints. Paths must be smooth, efficient, and safe. Visualization of configuration spaces helps explain how high-dimensional geometric problems are reduced to navigable representations.

These ideas connect geometry directly to robotics and autonomous systems.

Geometry in Graphics and Visualization

Computer graphics depend fundamentally on geometric algorithms. Rendering scenes requires determining which objects are visible, how surfaces intersect with light, and how shapes project onto screens.

Geometric transformations, intersection tests, and spatial hierarchies allow graphics systems to render complex scenes efficiently. Without these algorithms, modern visualization, gaming, and simulation would be impossible.

Geographic Information Systems

Geographic information systems operate on massive spatial datasets. Roads, boundaries, land use regions, and elevation data all require geometric processing.

Algorithms determine whether a location lies within a region, how routes intersect, and how spatial features relate. These systems demonstrate that computational geometry scales not only in dimension, but in data volume.

Numerical Robustness and Precision

Geometric algorithms are particularly sensitive to numerical precision. Small rounding errors can lead to incorrect decisions about intersections or containment.

Practical computational geometry therefore emphasizes robustness. Algorithms are designed to minimize numerical instability and handle degenerate cases gracefully. This engineering discipline is as important as mathematical correctness.

Reflection: Thinking in Space

Computational geometry teaches a distinct way of thinking. It encourages you to reason visually, structurally, and spatially, while remaining precise and algorithmic. It bridges the gap between abstract computation and the physical world.

With this chapter, the book completes its exploration of algorithmic domains, from numbers and strings to networks, learning systems, and spatial reasoning. Together, these chapters form a unified view of algorithms as tools for understanding, modeling, and shaping the world around us.

21. Algorithms in Operating Systems

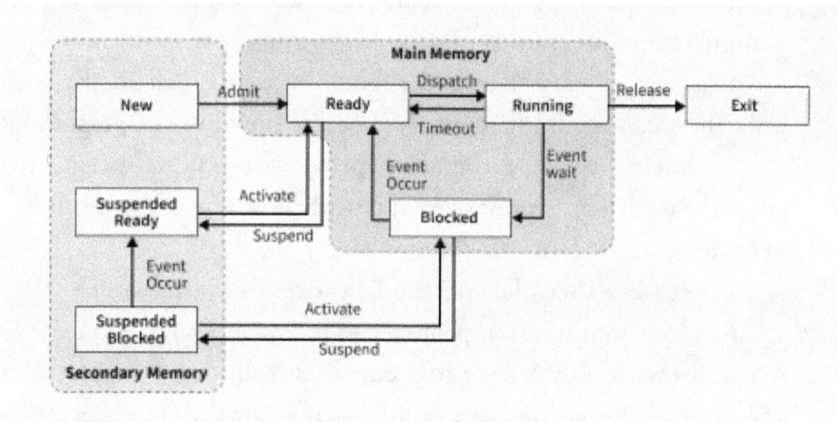

When you open an application, switch between windows, save a file, or connect to a network, it feels instantaneous and effortless. Beneath this smooth experience lies a dense web of algorithms making constant decisions about time, memory, storage, and fairness. Operating systems are among the most algorithmically rich pieces of software ever built, not because they use exotic techniques, but because they must apply algorithms continuously, reliably, and under strict constraints.

This chapter reveals the hidden algorithms that keep computers responsive and stable. Rather than treating operating systems as mysterious black boxes, we examine them as **practical engineering systems shaped by algorithmic choices**. Scheduling, memory management, and resource allocation are presented not as abstract theory, but as design decisions that directly affect performance, responsiveness, and user experience. A detailed look at the Linux scheduler grounds these ideas in a real, widely used system.

Why Operating Systems Are Algorithmic at Heart

An operating system sits between hardware and applications, mediating access to limited resources. CPU time, memory, disk bandwidth, and network capacity must be shared among many competing processes. The operating system cannot satisfy all requests simultaneously, so it must decide *who gets what, when, and for how long.*

These decisions are made by algorithms. Unlike one-off computations, operating system algorithms run continuously. They must be fast, predictable, and robust, because small inefficiencies or unfairness can accumulate into noticeable slowdowns or instability.

Operating systems therefore provide a unique perspective on algorithms. They emphasize practicality, tradeoffs, and long-term behavior over elegant one-time solutions.

Processes, Threads, and the Illusion of Parallelism

Modern computers appear to run many programs at once, even on machines with only a few CPU cores. This illusion is created through **scheduling algorithms** that rapidly switch the CPU between tasks.

A process represents a running program with its own memory space, while threads represent units of execution within a process. The operating system scheduler decides which thread runs at any given moment, how long it runs, and when it should be paused.

From an algorithmic standpoint, scheduling is a constrained optimization problem. The system must balance responsiveness, throughput, fairness, and priority, often with incomplete information about future behavior.

CPU Scheduling: Deciding Who Runs Next

FCFS:

Non-preemptive SJF:

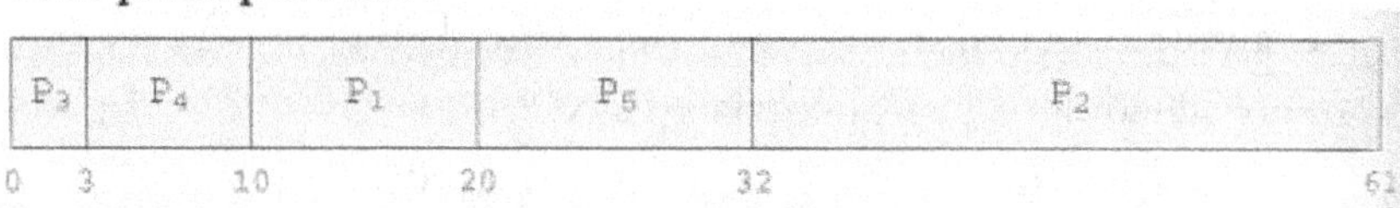

Round Robin:

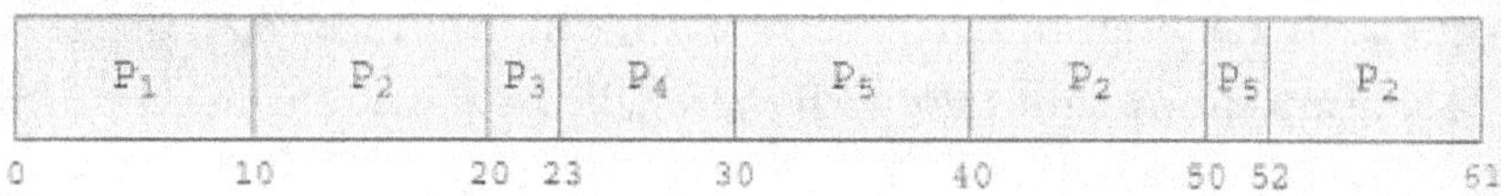

At the core of multitasking lies CPU scheduling. The simplest scheduling strategy runs tasks in the order they arrive. While easy to implement, this approach performs poorly when tasks vary in length, because short tasks may wait behind long ones.

More sophisticated schedulers attempt to share CPU time more equitably or favor interactive tasks that need quick responses. Scheduling algorithms therefore encode assumptions about workload behavior and user expectations.

Gantt charts are especially useful here. They visually represent how CPU time is divided among tasks, making tradeoffs between fairness and efficiency immediately visible.

Preemption and Time Slicing

Most modern operating systems use preemptive scheduling, where the scheduler can interrupt a running task to give another task a chance to run. This interruption occurs through time slicing, where each task receives a small-time quantum.

Time slicing introduces overhead, but it dramatically improves responsiveness. Interactive applications remain usable even when background tasks are consuming significant CPU resources.

Algorithmically, preemption transforms scheduling into a dynamic, feedback-driven process rather than a static queue.

The Linux Scheduler: A Real-World Case Study

The Linux operating system, developed by a global community and used in servers, desktops, and embedded systems, provides a compelling example of scheduler design. The **Linux** kernel uses the Completely Fair Scheduler, often abbreviated as CFS.

Rather than relying on fixed priorities alone, CFS models scheduling as a fairness problem. Each task accumulates virtual runtime based on how much processor time it has received. The scheduler always chooses the task with the smallest virtual runtime, ensuring that no task is starved over time.

This approach reflects a clear algorithmic philosophy. Instead of predicting task behavior, the scheduler reacts to observed execution history, producing balanced long-term outcomes.

Why Fairness Is an Algorithmic Choice

Fairness is not a single concept. Fairness can mean equal CPU time, equal responsiveness, or equal progress toward completion. Different systems and workloads require different interpretations.

The Linux scheduler's design demonstrates how algorithmic choices embody values. By prioritizing fairness over strict priority, Linux aims to provide consistent performance across diverse workloads, from interactive desktops to high-throughput servers.

Understanding this philosophy helps explain why operating system behavior varies across platforms and configurations.

Memory Management: Algorithms for Limited Space

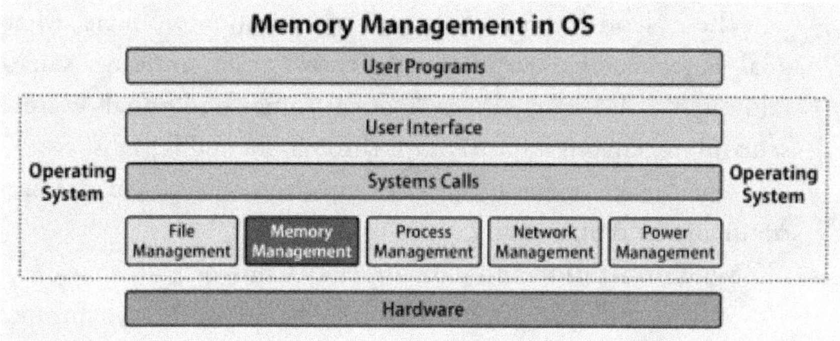

Memory is another scarce resource that must be managed algorithmically. Applications assume they have access to large, contiguous memory spaces, even though physical memory is limited.

Operating systems solve this problem through **virtual memory**, which maps virtual addresses used by programs to physical memory locations. Paging algorithms decide which memory pages remain in RAM and which are moved to disk when space runs low.

These algorithms must predict future memory access patterns based on past behavior, a challenge that echoes caching and approximation strategies discussed earlier in this book.

Page Replacement Algorithms

When physical memory fills up, the operating system must decide which page to evict. Simple strategies remove the oldest page, while more advanced algorithms attempt to remove pages that are unlikely to be used again soon.

Although perfect prediction is impossible, practical algorithms approximate it effectively. The success of virtual memory depends not on perfect decisions, but on making *good enough* choices consistently.

Memory diagrams help illustrate how pages move between RAM and disk, making abstract replacement decisions tangible.

Disk Scheduling and I/O Algorithms

Accessing disk storage is far slower than accessing memory. Disk scheduling algorithms attempt to minimize seek time by ordering read and write requests intelligently.

These algorithms resemble path optimization problems, where the goal is to service requests efficiently while avoiding starvation. Although solid-state drives reduce some traditional constraints, scheduling remains important for throughput and fairness.

Once again, operating system algorithms reflect a balance between optimality and practicality.

Synchronization and Concurrency Control

When multiple threads access shared data, synchronization algorithms prevent conflicts and corruption. Locks, semaphores, and atomic operations enforce ordering constraints that preserve correctness.

These algorithms must be carefully designed to avoid deadlocks, lovelocks, and performance bottlenecks. Small mistakes in synchronization logic can have catastrophic consequences, making correctness paramount.

Concurrency algorithms demonstrate that correctness and performance are often in tension, requiring disciplined design.

How OS Algorithms Shape User Experience

The impact of operating system algorithms is felt directly by users. Slow scheduling leads to laggy interfaces. Poor memory management causes thrashing. Inefficient I/O scheduling results in long load times.

Conversely, well-designed algorithms create the impression that hardware is faster and more capable than it really is. Operating systems succeed when their algorithms fade into the background.

OS Algorithm Summary

Operating systems rely on scheduling algorithms to share CPU time, memory management algorithms to extend limited resources, synchronization algorithms to preserve correctness, and I/O algorithms to optimize access to slow devices. Each of these algorithmic families reflects engineering tradeoffs shaped by workload assumptions and performance goals.

This summary serves as a reminder that operating systems are not collections of tricks, but coherent algorithmic systems.

Reflection: Algorithms You Never See

Operating system algorithms rarely receive attention because they work best when unnoticed. Yet they are among the most important algorithms you will ever depend on. They determine how efficiently your hardware is used, how responsive your applications feel, and how stable your system remains under load.

By understanding these hidden algorithms, you gain a deeper appreciation for the role of algorithmic thinking in everyday computing. Algorithms are not only tools for solving isolated problems. They are the invisible infrastructure that makes modern digital life possible.

22. Streaming and Online Algorithms

Much of classical algorithm design assumes that all data is available in advance, stored neatly in memory, and ready to be processed multiple times. Modern computing increasingly violates every one of these assumptions. Data now arrives continuously, at high speed, and often without a clear endpoint. In this environment, algorithms must make decisions **in real time**, with limited memory, and often without knowing what data will arrive next. Streaming and online algorithms are designed precisely for this reality.

This chapter introduces algorithmic thinking under immediacy and constraint. Instead of asking how to compute the best possible answer given unlimited time and space, we ask how to compute a useful answer *now*, using only a small amount of memory, while data continues to flow. Through concrete examples and a social-media case study, you will see how space–time tradeoffs become central design concerns and why approximation and probabilistic thinking often become necessities rather than choices.

From Stored Data to Data in Motion

Traditional offline algorithms operate on static datasets. They can sort the data, scan it multiple times, and revisit earlier decisions. Streaming algorithms operate under very different conditions. Data arrives one element at a time, possibly at millions of events per second, and storing the entire stream is either impractical or impossible.

In streaming contexts, algorithms must process each data item quickly, often in constant or logarithmic time, and then either discard it or retain only a carefully chosen summary. This shift forces a fundamental change in mindset. Memory becomes a scarce resource, and decisions are often irreversible.

What Makes an Algorithm Online

An online algorithm makes decisions without full knowledge of future input. Each decision is based only on what has been seen so far.

This contrasts with offline algorithms, which can examine the entire input before acting.

Online algorithms appear naturally in scheduling, caching, and real-time control systems. Streaming algorithms are a specific class of online algorithms that focus on continuous data flows. Both require reasoning under uncertainty, where future inputs may invalidate earlier assumptions.

Understanding this distinction clarifies why optimality is often redefined in online settings. Instead of absolute optimality, we measure competitiveness or approximation quality relative to an ideal algorithm with full knowledge.

The Central Constraint: Limited Memory

The defining constraint of streaming algorithms is memory. If a data stream contains billions of elements, storing them all defeats the purpose of streaming. Algorithms must therefore operate using memory that is sublinear in the size of the stream, often dramatically so.

This limitation leads to clever summaries. Instead of storing raw data, algorithms store counts, sketches, samples, or compressed representations. These summaries sacrifice detail to preserve essential information, enabling meaningful computation under tight constraints.

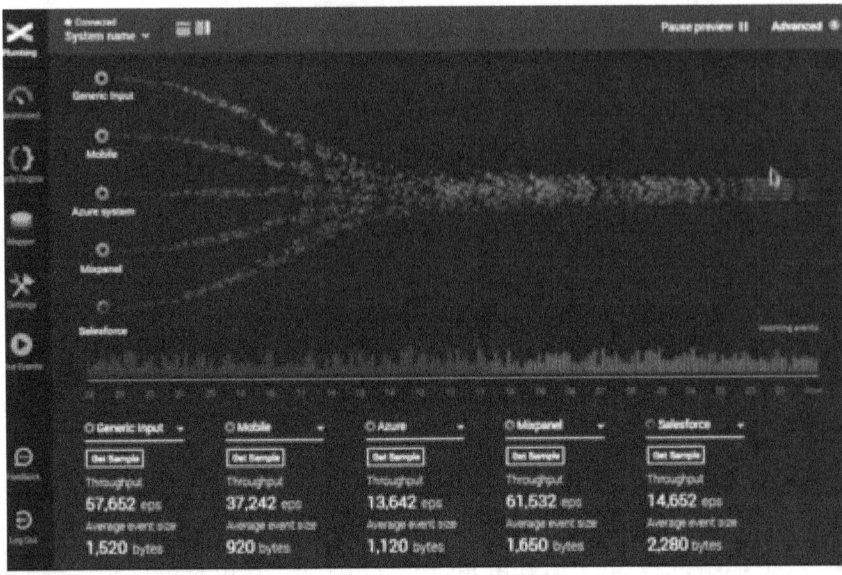

A Simple Example: Counting in a Stream

Consider counting how many times each item appears in a stream. If the stream is small, this is trivial. If the stream is massive and unbounded, exact counting may be infeasible.

Streaming algorithms address this by approximating frequencies. They may track only the most frequent items, or maintain probabilistic data structures that estimate counts with bounded error. These approaches demonstrate a recurring theme: exact answers are often replaced with statistically reliable approximations.

Time Matters Too

In addition to memory constraints, streaming algorithms face strict time constraints. Each data item must be processed quickly enough to keep up with the stream. Falling behind means losing data or increasing latency.

This requirement explains why streaming algorithms are often simple in structure. Complex computation is replaced with constant-time updates and lightweight data structures. The challenge lies in deciding what information is worth keeping and what can be safely forgotten.

Twitter Trends: A Case Study in Real Time

Social media platforms provide a vivid example of streaming algorithms in action. On **Twitter**, millions of posts arrive every minute, reflecting conversations happening around the world. Identifying trending topics requires analyzing this stream in real time.

The system cannot store and reprocess every message repeatedly. Instead, it maintains summaries that track emerging patterns, such as rapidly increasing word frequencies or unusual bursts of activity. These summaries are updated continuously as new data arrives.

This case study illustrates why immediacy matters. Trends lose value if they are detected too late. Streaming algorithms succeed by prioritizing speed and relevance over perfect accuracy.

Sliding Windows and Recent History

Many streaming problems care more about recent data than about the distant past. Sliding window models capture this idea by focusing on the most recent portion of the stream, such as the last minute, hour, or day.

Algorithms designed for sliding windows must update summaries as new data enters and old data expires. This requirement introduces additional complexity, but it reflects real-world needs, where recency often matters more than completeness.

Approximation and Probabilistic Guarantees

Because streaming algorithms operate under tight constraints, approximation is not a weakness but a design principle. Algorithms provide guarantees such as "the estimate is within a small error margin with high probability."

Probabilistic reasoning plays a central role here. Random sampling, hashing, and sketching techniques allow algorithms to maintain useful summaries while using very little memory. These techniques connect directly to randomized algorithms and approximation strategies discussed earlier in the book.

Streaming in the Internet of Things

The Internet of Things produces continuous streams of sensor data from devices embedded in homes, factories, cities, and vehicles. Temperature readings, motion detection, energy usage, and health metrics all arrive as streams that must be processed in real time.

Streaming algorithms enable anomaly detection, monitoring, and control without overwhelming storage systems. Decisions such as triggering alerts or adjusting behavior must be made immediately, often at the edge rather than in centralized data centers.

This context highlights how streaming algorithms support responsiveness and scalability simultaneously.

Space–Time Tradeoffs in Practice

Streaming algorithms embody some of the clearest space–time tradeoffs in computer science. Using less memory often means accepting more error. Using more computation per item may reduce error but increase latency.

Designing effective streaming algorithms therefore requires balancing these competing goals deliberately. There is rarely a single best solution, only solutions that fit particular constraints and priorities.

Streaming Algorithm Patterns

Several common patterns appear across streaming algorithms. One pattern involves maintaining small summaries that are updated incrementally. Another relies on sampling to represent large populations approximately. A third uses hashing to distribute information compactly across limited memory.

Recognizing these patterns helps you design streaming solutions even when facing unfamiliar problems. The details may change, but the underlying strategies recur.

Online Decision-Making and Adaptation

Streaming and online algorithms often operate in environments that change over time. User behavior shifts, sensors drift, and workloads evolve. Algorithms must therefore adapt continuously rather than converge to a fixed solution.

This adaptive behavior aligns streaming algorithms closely with machine learning systems, where models are updated incrementally as new data arrives. The boundary between streaming computation and learning is increasingly blurred in modern systems.

When Streaming Is the Right Model

Streaming algorithms are appropriate when data arrives continuously, when storing all data is impractical, and when timely responses are more valuable than perfect accuracy. They are less suitable when exact answers are required or when data can be processed offline without urgency.

Recognizing these conditions prevents misuse and guides appropriate algorithm selection.

Reflection: Thinking in Flows Instead of Files

Streaming and online algorithms teach a distinctive form of algorithmic thinking. They encourage you to think in terms of flows rather than datasets, summaries rather than storage, and responsiveness rather than completeness.

As computing systems become increasingly real time, distributed, and data driven, this way of thinking grows ever more important. Streaming algorithms remind us that algorithms are not just about computing answers, but about making timely decisions in a world that never stops producing data.

23. Algorithm Ethics and Societal Impact

Algorithms no longer operate quietly in the background of technical systems alone. They increasingly participate in decisions that shape human lives, influencing who is hired, who receives credit, how long a sentence might be, which medical treatment is prioritized, and what information people see or never encounter. As algorithms gain this power, questions of responsibility, fairness, and accountability move from philosophy seminars into everyday engineering practice.

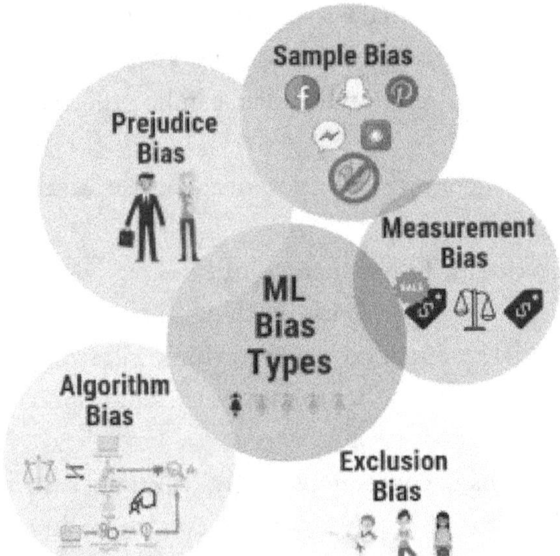

This chapter approaches algorithm ethics without easy answers or moral shortcuts. Ethical challenges in algorithms are rarely caused by malicious intent. They arise from design choices, data limitations, institutional pressures, and mismatches between technical optimization and human values. By examining real controversies and grounding ethical concerns in algorithmic mechanisms, this chapter encourages careful, critical thinking rather than superficial compliance.

Why Ethics Is an Algorithmic Concern

It is tempting to frame ethics as something external to algorithms, a matter for policymakers or legal teams rather than engineers. This framing is misleading. Ethical consequences often emerge directly from algorithmic design decisions such as choice of objective function, selection of training data, definition of success metrics, and tolerance for error.

Algorithms formalize priorities. When an algorithm optimizes efficiency, accuracy, or profit, it inevitably deprioritizes other values. These tradeoffs are not neutral. They encode assumptions about what outcomes matter and for whom. Understanding this connection is the first step toward responsible algorithm design.

From Technical Choices to Social Outcomes

Every algorithm simplifies reality. It reduces complex human situations into inputs, outputs, and measurable signals. This simplification is necessary for computation, but it creates blind spots. Characteristics that are difficult to quantify, such as potential, context, or structural disadvantage, are often excluded.

When algorithms operate at scale, these blind spots become systemic. Small biases, tolerable in isolation, accumulate into patterns that affect entire populations. Ethical impact therefore cannot be assessed by looking at individual cases alone. It must be evaluated at the level of systems and long-term effects.

Bias: Not Just a Data Problem

Algorithmic bias is often described as a data problem, and data certainly plays a central role. Historical data reflects historical inequalities. When algorithms learn from that data, they risk reproducing and amplifying those inequalities.

However, bias is not only about data. It also arises from modeling choices. Deciding which variables to include, how to define categories, and how to measure success shapes outcomes. Even well-intentioned efforts to remove sensitive attributes can fail, because correlated variables may act as proxies.

Understanding bias requires both technical insight and social awareness. It is not enough to ask whether an algorithm is accurate. One must ask *for whom* it is accurate and *at what cost*.

Hiring Algorithms: Opportunity at Stake

Automated hiring systems illustrate how algorithmic bias becomes a life-changing issue. Resume screening algorithms aim to identify promising candidates efficiently, but they often rely on historical hiring data that reflects past preferences and exclusions.

High-profile cases, including internal tools developed by **Amazon**, have shown how algorithms can inadvertently penalize certain groups because the data encodes patterns of past inequality. The algorithm does not "intend" to discriminate, yet its outcomes do.

This example demonstrates that removing explicit bias is not sufficient. Ethical algorithm design requires examining feedback loops, institutional context, and downstream effects.

Algorithms in the Justice System

Risk assessment algorithms used in bail and sentencing decisions raise particularly serious ethical concerns. These systems attempt to predict the likelihood of reoffending or failing to appear in court, often using demographic and historical data.

When such predictions influence incarceration decisions, errors are not abstract. They affect freedom, family stability, and future opportunity. Debates around these systems highlight tensions between efficiency, public safety, and individual rights.

These controversies reveal that algorithmic "objectivity" is often an illusion. Algorithms do not escape moral judgment simply because they are mathematical.

Credit Scoring and Financial Access

Credit scoring algorithms determine access to loans, housing, and economic mobility. While automation enables scale and consistency, it can also entrench disadvantage if historical inequities are treated as predictive truths rather than social artifacts.

Credit decisions illustrate a broader ethical dilemma. Systems designed to minimize financial risk may conflict with societal goals of inclusion and opportunity. Deciding how to balance these goals is not a purely technical question, yet algorithms force that balance into concrete operational form.

Privacy: Data as a Moral Boundary

Many ethical issues stem from how data is collected, stored, and reused. Algorithms often rely on large volumes of personal data, sometimes gathered without meaningful consent or understanding.

Privacy concerns are not only about secrecy. They are about control, autonomy, and dignity. When individuals cannot predict or influence how their data is used, power shifts toward institutions and away from individuals.

Algorithm designers play a role here by deciding what data is truly necessary, how long it should be retained, and how transparently its use can be explained.

Transparency and Explainability

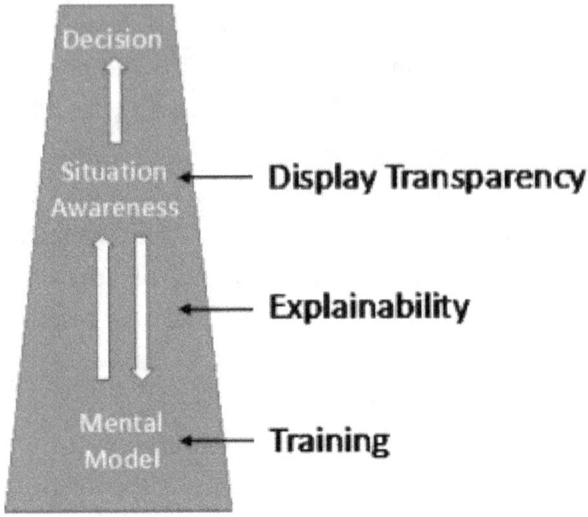

Transparency is frequently proposed as a solution to ethical concerns, yet it is more complex than it appears. Simply revealing source code or model parameters rarely helps affected individuals understand decisions that impact them.

Meaningful transparency focuses on explanations that are appropriate to the audience. A system that affects loan approval should be able to explain, in human terms, why a particular outcome occurred and how it might change. This requirement has algorithmic implications, influencing model choice and system architecture.

Explainability is therefore not an afterthought. It is a design constraint.

Accountability in Algorithmic Systems

When algorithms make harmful decisions, responsibility can become diffuse. Designers blame data. Organizations blame tools. Tools are treated as neutral artifacts. This diffusion of responsibility is itself an ethical failure.

Responsible systems establish clear lines of accountability. They define who can challenge decisions, who can override them, and who bears responsibility for harm. Algorithms that cannot be audited or contested undermine trust, regardless of their technical sophistication.

Ethical Decision Frameworks

Ethical decision frameworks help structure thinking without providing automatic answers. They encourage designers to ask systematic questions about stakeholders, risks, benefits, and alternatives.

Visual frameworks emphasize that ethical evaluation is iterative. As systems evolve, new risks emerge. Ethics is not a one-time checklist, but an ongoing process integrated into development and deployment.

The Ethical Algorithm Checklist

Before deploying an algorithm that affects people's lives, it is worth pausing to ask critical questions. Who benefits and who bears risk. What assumptions are embedded in the data. How are errors handled and who is harmed when they occur. Can decisions be explained and contested. Are there feedback loops that may amplify harm over time.

This checklist does not guarantee ethical outcomes, but it promotes deliberate reflection rather than unexamined automation.

Tradeoffs Without Simple Answers

Ethical algorithm design rarely offers clean solutions. Improving fairness may reduce accuracy by some metrics. Enhancing privacy may limit performance. Increasing transparency may expose systems to manipulation.

These tradeoffs are unavoidable. The ethical challenge lies not in eliminating them, but in making them explicit and choosing responsibly. Pretending that algorithms are neutral avoids the hard work of value-based decision making.

A Life-Changing Decisions Case Study

Consider an algorithm that determines eligibility for social services, medical prioritization, or parole. Each decision is informed by probabilities and thresholds. Each decision also intersects with human vulnerability.

This case study forces a difficult question. Even if an algorithm improves average outcomes, is it acceptable if it causes severe harm in a small number of cases. Different societies, institutions, and individuals will answer differently. Algorithms do not remove this moral burden. They concentrate it.

Reflection: Designing with Moral Awareness

Algorithm ethics is not about turning engineers into philosophers, nor about halting innovation. It is about recognizing that algorithms are forms of power. They shape opportunities, distribute risk, and encode values into automated processes.

By approaching algorithm design with moral awareness, engineers and decision makers can move beyond the false comfort of neutrality. They can design systems that are not only efficient and scalable, but also worthy of the trust placed in them.

24. The Future of Algorithms

Algorithms have always evolved alongside the limits and possibilities of computation. What began as hand-executed procedures for arithmetic now governs global communication networks, autonomous machines, and decision-making systems that affect billions of people. Looking toward the future of algorithms therefore requires both imagination and restraint. Imagination helps us see what might be possible. Restraint keeps us grounded in what is actually known, what remains uncertain, and what responsibility accompanies progress.

This final chapter looks forward without speculation for its own sake. It connects emerging technologies to the algorithmic ideas developed throughout this book and highlights open problems that remain unsolved. The aim is not to predict the future perfectly, but to prepare you to participate in it thoughtfully, critically, and confidently.

Why the Future of Algorithms Matters

Algorithms shape how societies function. They influence efficiency, fairness, security, creativity, and access to information. As computational systems expand into new domains, the consequences of algorithmic design choices grow in scope and permanence.

The future of algorithms is not only about faster computation or smarter systems. It is about *what kinds of problems we choose to automate*, *how we encode values into systems*, and *who benefits from algorithmic progress*. These questions ensure that the future of algorithms remains as much a human challenge as a technical one.

Trends That Are Already Shaping Tomorrow

Several forces are already redefining algorithm design. Data volumes continue to grow, pushing algorithms toward streaming, approximation, and distributed execution. Hardware diversity increases, with CPUs, GPUs, specialized accelerators, and edge devices coexisting within the same systems. Uncertainty becomes the norm, not the exception, encouraging probabilistic, adaptive, and learning-based approaches.

Rather than replacing classical algorithms, these trends expand the design space. Foundational ideas such as divide and conquer, dynamic programming, and greedy choice continue to appear, but they are embedded within larger, more complex systems.

Quantum Computing: A New Computational Model

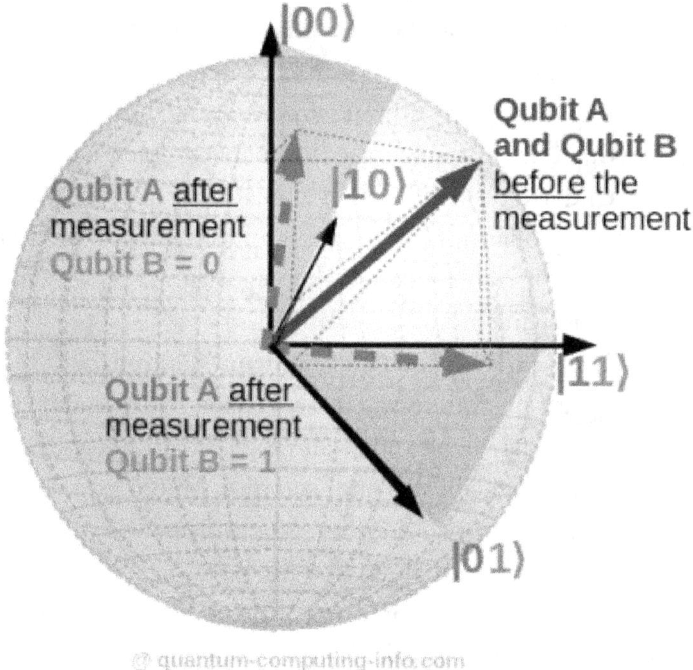

Quantum computing represents one of the most profound potential shifts in algorithmic thinking. Instead of classical bits that are either zero or one, quantum computers operate on quantum bits that can exist in superpositions of states. This property allows certain computations to explore many possibilities simultaneously.

Quantum algorithms do not simply run faster versions of classical algorithms. They exploit entirely different physical principles. Some problems that appear intractable on classical machines may become feasible, while others see little or no benefit.

Importantly, quantum computing does not make all hard problems easy. Its power is specialized, not universal.

Quantum Algorithms Without Intimidation

One of the most famous quantum algorithms is Shor's algorithm, which factors large integers efficiently on a quantum computer. This capability has major implications for cryptography, because it threatens systems that rely on the difficulty of factoring.

Another example, Grover's algorithm, provides a quadratic speedup for unstructured search problems. While impressive, this speedup does not magically eliminate complexity; it reshapes it.

Understanding quantum algorithms conceptually does not require mastering quantum physics. It requires recognizing that computation itself can be redefined, and that algorithmic power depends deeply on the underlying model of computation.

The Reality Check on Quantum Computing

Quantum computing remains an active research area rather than a mature, widely deployed technology. Practical challenges such as error correction, scalability, and stability limit current systems. For the foreseeable future, quantum algorithms will complement classical algorithms rather than replace them.

This reality reinforces an important lesson. Algorithmic futures unfold gradually. Breakthroughs are real, but they coexist with long periods of refinement, hybrid systems, and partial adoption.

Algorithms and Artificial Intelligence Co-Evolving

Machine learning and artificial intelligence continue to influence algorithm design profoundly. Algorithms increasingly adapt over time, learn from feedback, and operate under uncertainty. At the same time, classical algorithmic ideas are being rediscovered and repurposed within learning systems.

Optimization, graph algorithms, and probabilistic reasoning appear repeatedly inside modern AI pipelines. The future is not a clean divide between "traditional algorithms" and "AI," but a convergence where learning and algorithmic structure reinforce each other.

Algorithms at the Edge

As computation moves closer to where data is generated, such as sensors, mobile devices, and embedded systems, algorithms must operate under tighter constraints. Limited power, limited memory, and real-time requirements reshape design priorities.

Edge algorithms favor simplicity, robustness, and approximate reasoning. They often rely on local decisions with occasional global coordination. This trend emphasizes that future algorithms will not live only in data centers, but everywhere computation touches the physical world.

Security, Privacy, and Trust as Algorithmic Frontiers

Future algorithms must operate in environments where trust cannot be assumed. Adversarial behavior, data poisoning, and manipulation are not edge cases. They are design constraints.

Algorithms that can reason about uncertainty, detect anomalies, and preserve privacy will become increasingly important. Cryptography, secure computation, and privacy-preserving algorithms are therefore not niche topics, but central pillars of future systems.

Open Problems That Still Matter

Despite decades of progress, some of the most important algorithmic questions remain open. Whether efficient exact algorithms exist for certain classes of problems is still unknown. How to design algorithms that are provably fair, explainable, and robust at scale remains an active area of research.

There are also open challenges in energy-efficient computation, resilient distributed systems, and algorithms that can align with human values more reliably. These problems are not merely technical. They are interdisciplinary by nature.

The future of algorithms is shaped as much by what we *do not yet know* as by what we already understand.

Opportunities Beyond Traditional Boundaries

Algorithms increasingly influence domains once considered outside computer science. Biology, economics, climate modeling, law, and the arts all engage with algorithmic systems. These intersections create opportunities for new kinds of algorithms, informed by domain knowledge and ethical considerations.

The most impactful future algorithms may come not from deeper specialization alone, but from thoughtful collaboration across disciplines.

Your Learning Journey: A Roadmap Forward

Learning algorithms is not a finite task. It is a continuous process of refinement and curiosity. A strong foundation in problem solving, data structures, and complexity analysis prepares you to adapt as technologies evolve.

From there, exploring specialized areas such as distributed systems, learning algorithms, security, or computational geometry allows you to deepen expertise while staying connected to core principles. Reading research, building systems, and reflecting on real-world impact all contribute to growth.

This journey rewards patience and humility. Even experienced researchers regularly revisit fundamentals.

Staying Grounded While Looking Ahead

Future-focused thinking can easily drift into hype or fear. Responsible algorithmic thinking resists both. It evaluates new ideas critically, tests assumptions empirically, and considers consequences carefully.

Progress in algorithms has always been incremental, collaborative, and iterative. Breakthroughs are built on layers of prior insight. By understanding this history, you gain confidence that the future is navigable rather than overwhelming.

A Final Reflection: Algorithms as Human Tools

Algorithms are not destiny. They are tools created by people, shaped by choices, and embedded within social systems. Their future depends on how thoughtfully they are designed, applied, and governed.

As you close this book, you are not reaching an endpoint. You are acquiring a lens through which to see problems more clearly and systems more deeply. Whether you design algorithms, use them, or shape policies around them, your understanding matters.

The future of algorithms is not something that simply happens. It is something we build, question, and refine together.

www.ingramcontent.com/pod-product-compliance
Lightning Source LLC
LaVergne TN
LVHW022052200926
848481LV00003B/874